World Link | Developing English Fluency

INTRO

Susan Stempleski

James R. Morgan • Nancy Douglas

HEINLE
CENGAGE Learning

Australia • Brazil • Japan • Korea • Mexico • Singapore • Spain • United Kingdom • United States

HEINLE
CENGAGE Learning

World Link Intro, **Student Book**
Susan Stempleski
Nancy Douglas, James R. Morgan

Publisher: Christopher Wenger
Director of Content Development:
Anita Raducanu
Director of Product Marketing: Amy Mabley
Acquisitions Editor: Mary Sutton-Paul
Sr. Marketing Manager: Eric Bredenberg
Developmental Editor: Paul MacIntyre
Developmenttal Editor: Sally Cogliano
Content Project Manager: Tan Jin Hock
Sr. Print Buyer: Mary Beth Hennebury
Compositor: CHROME Media Pte. Ltd.
Project Manager: Christopher Hanzie
Photography Manager: Sheri Blaney
Photo Researcher: Christopher Hanzie
Illustrator: Raketshop Design Studio
(Philippines), Melvin Chong (Singapore),
Meredith Morgan (U.S.A.)
Cover/Text Designer: CHROME Media Pte. Ltd.
Cover Images: CHROME Media Pte. Ltd.,
PhotoDisc, Inc.

Photo Credits

Unless otherwise stated, all photos are from PhotoDisc, Inc. Digital Imagery © copyright 2005 PhotoDisc, Inc. and TYA Inc. Photos from other sources: page 3: (top) Royalty-Free/CORBIS, (middle) Heinle, (bottom) Patricia Barry Levy / Index Stock Imagery; page 6: Alan Schein Photography/CORBIS; page 7: (C. Aguilera) MIKE BLAKE/Reuters/Landov, (K. Reeves) MIKE BLAKE/Reuters/Landov, (A. Agassi) DAVID GRAY/Reuters/Landov, (M. Yeoh) CLARO CORTES IV/Reuters/Landov; page 8: (J. Lopez) PETER FOLEY/Landov, (Eminem) GARY HERSHORN/Reuters /Landov, (J. Li) KIN CHEUNG/Reuters /Landov, (J. Aniston) MICHAEL GERMANA/UPI /Landov, (T. Woods) TOBY MELVILLE/Reuters /Landov, (Ronaldo) BRUNO DOMINGOS/Reuters /Landov; page 8: (Marilyn Monroe) DPA /Landov; page 9: (J. Lopez) HUBERT BOESL/dpa /Landov, (J. Li) ADREES LATIF/Reuters /Landov, (Ronaldo) SERGIO PEREZ/Reuters /Landov, (J. Aniston) SÖREN STACHE/dpa /Landov; page 10: (Ahn Jung Hwan) Kyodo /Landov, YURIKO NAKAO/Reuters /Landov; page 11: (Norah Jones) SHAUN BEST/Reuters /Landov, (Tom Cruise) JOHN SCHULTS/Reuters /Landov; page 15: Vatican City; page 16: Heinle; page 17: Charles & Josette Lenars/CORBIS; page 24: Hemera Photo Objects; page 28: William Whitehurst/CORBIS, Comstock Images/Alamy, Hemera Photo Objects; page 35: (J. Timberlake) STEPHEN HIRD/Reuters /Landov, (J. Lopez) WOLFGANG LANGENSTRASSEN/dpa /Landov, (A. Jolie) MICHAEL GERMANA/UPI /Landov; page 39: AMET JEAN PIERRE/CORBIS SYGMA; page 51: Lou Jones / Index Stock Imagery Washington, Catherine Karnow/CORBIS; page 53: Hanan Isachar/CORBIS Gilroy, Robert Holmes/CORBIS; page 63: Jacques Langevin/CORBIS SYGMA; page 65: (Bono) TAMI CHAPPELL/Reuters /Landov, (Prince William) TOBY MELVILLE/Reuters /Landov, (Madonna) FRED PROUSER/Reuters /Landov, (Jackie Chan) KIN CHEUNG/Reuters /Landov, (Sean Connery) SOEREN STACHE/dpa /Landov, (Enrique Eglesias) ANDREA COMAS/Reuters /Landov; page 72: Jeremy Horner/CORBIS; page 74: RUSSELL BOYCE/Reuters/Landov, Twentieth Century FOX/The Everett Collection,Twentieth Century FOX, NBC/The Everett Collection; page 75: Image State/Alamy; page 76: Ed Kashi/CORBIS; page 81: (top) Alyx Kellington / Index Stock Imagery, (bottom) James Lemass / Index Stock Imagery; page 82: (C.Y. Fat) BOBBY YIP/REUTERS /Landov, (C. Diaz) FRED PROUSER/REUTERS /Landov, (J. Carrey) MICHAEL GERMANA/UPI /Landov, (Y. Ono) JEFF CHRISTENSEN/Reuters /Landov; page 86: Barry Lewis / Alamy, page 87: Henryk T. Kaiser / Index Stock Imagery, Charles & Josette Lenars/CORBIS; page 88: Paul Almasy/CORBIS; page 95: Peter Turnley/CORBIS; page 114: Fabrizio Cacciatore/Index Stock Immagery, John Henley/CORBIS; page 120: (Elizabeth of Russia) Bettmann/CORBIS; page 124: (J.K. Rowling) IAN WEST/EPA /Landov, (Alexander Graham Bell) (Ayrton Senna) Mike King/CORBIS, (Michael Flatley) Reuters /Landov, (Shakira) Reuters /Landov, (Frida Kahlo) Bettmann/CORBIS, (Will Smith) FRANCIS SPECKER Landov, (Jean Paul Gaultier) Justin Lane/EPA /Landov; page137: Bettmann/CORBIS

Every effort has been made to trace all sources of illustrations/photos/information in this book, but if any have been inadvertently overlooked, the publisher will be pleased to make the necessary arrangements at the first opportunity.

ISBN-13: 978-0-8384-0661-8

ISBN-10: 0-8384-0661-0

Heinle
20 Channel Center St.
Boston, MA 02210
USA

Cengage Learning is a leading provider of customized learning solutions with office locations around the globe, including Singapore, the United Kingdom, Australia, Mexico, Brazil and Japan. Locate our local office at: **international.cengage.com/region**

Cengage Learning products are represented in Canada by Nelson Education, Ltd.

Visit Heinle online at **elt.heinle.com**
Visit our corporate website at **cengage.com**

Printed in China by China Translation & Printing Services Limited
10 11 12 13 14 13 12 11 10

Acknowledgments

We would firstly like to thank the educators who provided invaluable feedback throughout the development of the *World Link* series:

Byung-kyoo Ahn, Chonnam National University; Elisabeth Blom, Casa Thomas Jefferson; Grazyna Anna Bonomi; Vera Burlamaqui Bradford, Instituto Brasil-Estados Unidos; Araceli Cabanillas Carrasco, Universidad Autónoma de Sinaloa; Silvania Capua Carvalho, State University of Feira de Santana; Tânia Branco Cavaignac, Casa Branca Idiomas; Kyung-whan Cha, Chung-Ang University; Chwun-li Chen, Shih Chien University; María Teresa Fátima Encinas, Universidad Iberoamericana-Puebla and Universidad Autónoma de Puebla; Sandra Gaviria, Universidad EAFIT; Marina González, Instituto de Lenguas Modernas; Frank Graziani, Tokai University; Chi-ying Fione Huang, Ming Chuan University; Shu-fen Huang (Jessie), Chung Hua University; Tsai, Shwu Hui (Ellen), Chung Kuo Institute of Technology and Commerce; Connie R. Johnson, Universidad de las Américas-Puebla; Diana Jones, Instituto Angloamericano; Annette Kaye, Kyoritsu Women's University; Lee, Kil-ryoung, Yeungnam University; David Kluge, Kinjo Gakuin University; Nancy H. Lake; Hyunoo Lee, Inha University; Amy Peijung Lee, Hsuan Chuang College; Hsiu-Yun Liao, Chinese Culture University; Yuh-Huey Gladys Lin, Chung Hua University; Eleanor Occeña, Universitaria de Idiomas, Universidad Autónoma del Estado de Hidalgo; Laura Pérez Palacio, Tecnológico de Monterrey; Doraci Perez Mak, União Cultural Brasil-Estados Unidos; Mae-Ran Park, Pukyong National University; Joo-Kyung Park, Honam University; Bill Pellowe, Kinki University; Margareth Perucci, Sociedade Brasileira de Cultura Inglesa; Nevitt Reagan, Kansai Gaidai University; Lesley D. Riley, Kanazawa Institute of Technology; Ramiro Luna Rivera, Tecnológico de Monterrey, Prepa; Marie Adele Ryan, Associação Alumni; Michael Shawback, Ritsumeikan University; Kathryn Singh, ITESM; Grant Trew, Nova Group; Michael Wu, Chung Hua University

---

A great many people participated in the making of the *World Link* series. In particular I would like to thank the authors, Nancy Douglas and James Morgan, for all their hard work, creativity, and good humor. I would also like to give special thanks to the developmental editor Paul MacIntyre, whose good judgment and careful attention to detail were invaluable. Thanks, too, to publisher Chris Wenger, and all the other wonderful people at Heinle who have worked on this project. I am also very grateful to the many reviewers around the world, whose insightful comments on early drafts of the *World Link* materials were much appreciated.

Susan Stempleski

We'd like to extend a very special thank you to two individuals at Heinle: Chris Wenger for spearheading the project and providing leadership, support and guidance throughout the development of the series, and Paul MacIntyre for his detailed and insightful editing, and his tireless commitment to this project. We also offer our sincere thanks to Susan Stempleski, whose extensive experience and invaluable feedback helped to shape the material in this book.

Thanks also go to those on the editorial, production, and support teams who helped to make this book happen: Anita Raducanu, Sally Cogliano, David Bohlke, Christine Galvin-Combet, Lisa Geraghty, Carmen Corral-Reid, Jean Pender, Rebecca Klevberg, Mary Sutton-Paul, and their colleagues in Asia and Latin America.

I would also like to thank my parents, Alexander and Patricia, for their love and encouragement. And to my husband Jorge and daughter Jasmine–thank you for your patience and faith in me. I couldn't have done this without you!
Nancy Douglas

Most importantly, I would like to thank my mother, Frances P. Morgan, for her unflagging support and my father, Lee Morgan Jr., for instilling the love of language and learning in me.
James R. Morgan

World Link Intro

Scope and Sequence

	Vocabulary Link	Listening	Speaking & Pronunciation
Unit 1 Greetings and Intros			
Lesson A 2 Getting to know you	Basic introductions *What's your name?, My name is . . .*	"My name is John.": Listening for names	"Meet your classmates!": Introducing yourself
Lesson B 7 People we like	*classmate, friend, family, boy/girlfriend;* various professions	"My friends call me Meg.": Listening for names and nicknames	Contractions with *be*
Unit 2 Countries and Nationalities			
Lesson A 12 Countries of the world	Countries and nationalities *Mexico, Mexican . . .*	"Are you from Japan?": Listening for countries and cities	"Where are you from?": Asking where someone is from
Lesson B 17 What is your city like?	Describing cities *big, crowded, noisy, beautiful, dirty . . .*	"What is L.A. like?": Listening for places and adjectives	Stressed syllables
Unit 3 Interesting Products			
Lesson A 22 Personal items	Personal items *laptop, watch, cell phone, purse, key . . .*	"A birthday gift": Listening for items and adjectives	"Is this your cell phone?": Saying *Thank you*
Lesson B 27 Modern electronics	Electronic items *camcorder, stereo, TV, MP3 player . . .*	"Is this your new DVD player?": Listening for items and opinions	Linking with *n*
Review: Units 1–3 32			
Unit 4 Activities and Interests			
Lesson A 36 Everyday activities	Common activities *listening to music, studying, eating . . .*	"What are you doing?": Listening for what people are doing	"How are you doing?": Asking how someone is (1)
Lesson B 41 At school	School subjects *writing, math, science, history...*	"I'm taking a math class.": Listening for class schedules	Question intonation
Unit 5 Food			
Lesson A 46 Food and eating habits	Foods for breakfast, lunch, and dinner;	"I'm making dinner.": Listening for foods drinks and desserts	"Do you like Italian food?": Talking about likes and dislikes
Lesson B 51 Food around the world	Describing festivals *festival, visit, traditional, parade . . .*	"Foods around the world": Listening for descriptions of food	*And*
Unit 6 My Family			
Lesson A 56 This is my family!	Family members *father, mother, son, daughter, sister...*	"Who is the speaker?": Listening for names and relationships	"Is this your family?" Asking and answering about family
Lesson B 61 Families, big and small	Family relationships *married, single, divorced . . .*	"Three families": Listening for personal details	Linking with *'s*
Review: Units 4–6 66			

Reading & Writing	Language Link	Communication
"Famous name changers": Reading about people's real names	Subject pronouns and possessive adjectives with *be*	"Nice to meet you!": Completing forms with personal information
"My web page": Making a web page	*Yes/No* questions and short answers with *be*	"My favorites": Asking and answering questions about favorites
		Unit 2
"A postcard from a friend": Reading a description of a place	Question words *where* and *who*	"The country and city game!": Asking and answering questions about places
"A postcard from my city": Describing a place	*Be* + adjective	"Vacation!": Choosing a vacation spot
		Unit 3
"Electronics for sale": Reading product reviews	Plurals; *this/that/these/those*	"Thanks a lot!": Giving and receiving gifts
"My product rating": Writing a product review	Adjectives and nouns	"Our favorite products": Designing and describing a new product
		Review: Units 1–3 32
		Unit 4
"What are you studying?": Reading a student interview	The present continuous	"What are they doing?": Comparing actions in two different pictures
"A student interview": Interviewing and writing about a partner	The present continuous: extended time	"Two truths and a lie": Talking about on-going activities
		Unit 5
"What's your favorite food festival?": Reading about international food festivals	The simple present	"The dinner party": Creating a seating chart for guests according to personal information.
"My favorite food": Writing about a favorite food	The simple present: *yes/no* questions and short answers	"Health habits and food customs": Taking and giving a health survey
		Unit 6
"How big is your family?": Reading family descriptions	Possessives	"My partner's family tree": Drawing a family tree
"About my family": Writing a letter about your family	Numbers 11–2,000	"Famous people": Giving information about famous people
		Review: Units 4–6 66

1 Vocabulary Link

What's your name?

A Complete the ID cards.
Use the class roster below.

Student ID

First name: Carlos

Last name: _____

E-mail address:

_____

Male __X__   Female _____

Student ID

First name: Mariko

Last name: ~~A~~ Akita _____

E-mail address:
marikoa@eazypost.com

Male _____   Female __X__

Student ID

First name: Liujun

Last name: _____

E-mail address:

_____

Male _____   Female __X__

Student ID

First name: _____

Last name: Cruz

E-mail address:

_____

Male __X__   Female _____

CLASS ROSTER

Semester: Spring **Course:** English 101
Teacher: Emily Whitman **Room:** 402

Last name	First name	E-mail address
Akita	Mariko	marikoa@eazypost.com
Ramalho	Carlos	Carlos@eazypost.com
Cruz	Francisco	Paco@starlink.net.mx
Wong	Liujun	wintermoon@sfu.edu

last name = family name

@ = "at"
.com = "dot com"
.edu = "dot e-d-u"
.net = "dot net"

  B Listen. Check your answers. (CD 1, Track 1)

 C Pair work. Ask a partner questions. Make an ID card for your partner.

What's your name?   *How do you spell that?*   *What's your e-mail address?*

2 Listening

My name is John.

 A **Listen. Fill in the blanks.** (CD 1, Track 2)

> 1. First name: <u> Koji </u>
>   Last name: _____
>   Male ☐ Female ☐

> 2. First name: _____
>   Last name: _____
>   Male ☐ Female ☐

> 3. First name: _____
>   Last name: _____
>   Male ☐ Female ☐

 B Pair work. **Say and spell the names in A with a partner.**

3 Pronunciation

Contractions with *be*

 A **Listen and repeat.** (CD 1, Track 3)

1. I am	I'm	4. he is	he's
2. you are	you're	5. it is	it's
3. she is	she's	6. what is	what's

 B **Listen and circle.** (CD 1, Track 4)

1. (I am) / I'm a teacher.
2. He is / He's my classmate.
3. You are / You're in my class.
4. She is / She's my partner.
5. Hi, Carlos. I am / I'm Anna.
6. What's your name? It is / It's John.

 C Pair work. **Practice saying the sentences in B with a partner.**

4 Speaking

Meet your classmates!

hi = hello

A Pair work. **Listen to the conversation. Then practice with a partner.** (CD 1, Track 5)

Mariko: Hi, my name is Mariko. What's your name?

Paco: Hi, Mariko. I'm Francisco, but please call me Paco. It's my nickname.

Mariko: Okay, Paco. Nice to meet you.

Paco: It's nice to meet you, too.

B **Complete this sentence with your name or nickname.**

In this class, please call me _____.

C Pair work. **Practice the conversation again with your partner. Use your own names.**

D Class activity. **Meet six classmates. Write your classmates' names in the box.**

My classmates

1. _____
2. _____
3. _____
4. _____
5. _____
6. _____

Useful Expressions:
Introducing yourself

Hi, what's your name?

My name is Mariko.
I'm Mariko.
I'm Frank Whitman.
My name is Sally Kim.

(It's) nice to meet you.

(It's) nice to meet you, too.

E Pair work. **Say your classmates' names to your partner.**

World Link

I'm Li Zhang. My last name is the most common in the world. There are more than 100 million Zhangs!

Subject pronouns and possessive adjectives with *be*

 Match each sentence with a picture.

a. **He is** a soccer player.
b. **You are** a student.
c. **It is** a book.
d. **I am** a student.
e. **She is** a student.

d

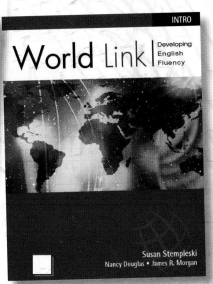

INTRO

World Link | Developing English Fluency

Susan Stempleski
Nancy Douglas • James R. Morgan

 **Complete the sentences. Use the words in the box.**

| Your | ~~My~~ | Its | Her | His |

1. **I am** a student. ___My___ name is Mariko.
2. **You are** a student. _____ teacher is Ms. Whitman.
3. **She is** a student. _____ name is Liujun.
4. **He is** a student. _____ name is Paco.
5. **It is** a book. _____ title is *World Link*.

Contractions with *be*

I am = I'm
you are = you're
she is = she's
he is = he's
it is = it's

 Pair work. Complete the conversation. Use contractions. Practice with a partner.

A: Hi. My name _____ _____. _____ a student in the class.
   What's _____ name?

B: _____ name _____ _____. _____ a student
   in the class, too. Nice to meet you.

A: nice to meet you, too.

6 Communication 💬

Nice to meet you!

Numbers 0–10

0	zero (oh)	4	four	8	eight
1	one	5	five	9	nine
2	two	6	six	10	ten
3	three	7	seven		

A Look at the answers. Write the questions.

1. What's _____?

   My name is Cristina Diaz.

2. _____?

   My e-mail address is CDiaz@eazypost.com.

3. _____?

   My phone number is (399) 555-7061.

B Imagine you are a new student at a school. Make up a new name, phone number, and e-mail address. Complete the form.

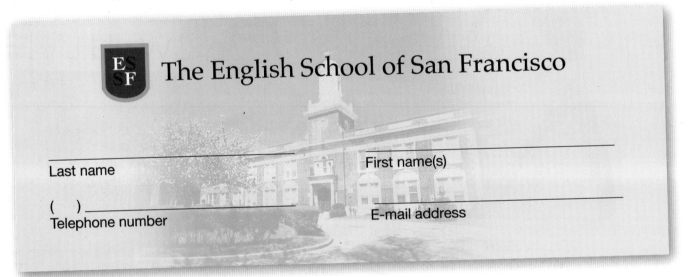

The English School of San Francisco

Last name _____   First name(s) _____

( ) _____   E-mail address _____
Telephone number

C Class activity. Meet four students. Write their information below. Remember to use your "new" name.

Student 1	Student 2
Last name: _____	Last name: _____
First name(s): _____	First name(s): _____
Phone number: _____	Phone number: _____
E-mail address: _____	E-mail address: _____

Student 3	Student 4
Last name: _____	Last name: _____
First name(s): _____	First name(s): _____
Phone number: _____	Phone number: _____
E-mail address: _____	E-mail address: _____

Greetings and Intros

Lesson B | People we like

1 Vocabulary Link

Friends and favorites

> *This is Meg. She's a university student in the United States.*

Gina

Meg

Tanya

Sam

Robert (father)
Clare (mother)
Tim (brother)

 A Look at the pictures. Complete the sentences. Use the words in the box.

> classmate   ~~boyfriend~~
> family   friend

1. Sam is Meg's ____boyfriend____.
2. Tanya is her _____.
3. Gina is her _____.
4. Robert, Clare, and Tim are her _____.

 B Pair work. Match the name to the picture. Tell a partner about each person.

a. Michelle Yeoh
b. Andre Agassi
c. Keanu Reeves
d. Christina Aguilera

singer

athlete

a

actress

actor

> *Michelle Yeoh is an actress.*

 C Pair work. Who are your favorites? Complete the sentences with your ideas. Tell your partner.

1. My favorite singer is _____.
2. My favorite athlete is _____.
3. My favorite actor is _____.
4. My favorite actress is _____.

2 Listening

My friends call me Meg.

 A Listen. Fill in the blanks with their names. (CD 1, Track 6)

1. Name: __Song Ling__   3. Name: _____
   Nickname: _____   Nickname: _____

2. Name: _____
   Nickname: _____

B Pair work. **Complete the sentences. Tell your partner.**

My name is _____ .
My family calls me _____ .
My friends call me _____ .
My classmates call me _____ .

World Link

The American actress Marilyn Monroe's real name was Norma Jeane Mortenson.

3 Reading

Famous name changers

Do you like your name?

 A Pair work. **Match a name with a photo. Check your answers with a partner.**

a. ~~Jennifer Aniston~~
b. Jet Li
c. Ronaldo
d. Eminem
e. Jennifer Lopez
f. Tiger Woods

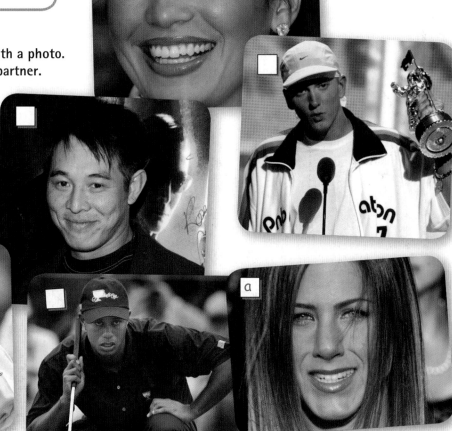

B Read. Write the people's names from **A** in the reading.

Famous Name Changers

1 She is an actress on the TV show *Friends*.
Is her real name _____?
No, it isn't. It's Jennifer Anistopoulou.

2 He's an athlete from Brazil. Everyone calls him by his
first name. His full name is _____
Luis Nazario de Lima.

3 His real name is Li Lian Jie. He is an actor and a martial
artist. His English name is _____.

4 He is a singer. His real name isn't _____.
It is Bruce Marshall Mathers.

5 She is a singer and an actress. Her full name is
_____.
Many people call her by her nickname, J. Lo.

6 He is an athlete. His name is Eldrick Woods, but people
call him by his nickname, _____.

C Pair work. Read again. Then point to the pictures in **A**. Tell
your partner about each person.

Her real name is Jennifer Anistopoulou.

ask&
ANSWER
Do you know a famous name changer?

Lesson B • People we like   **9**

4 Language Link

Yes/No questions and short answers with be

A Complete the chart with the questions and answers.

Yes, you are.	No, I'm not.	Is John a student?
Is your name Sara?	Yes, it is.	No, he's not. He's a teacher.

Yes/No Questions	Answers
Am I in this class?	1. ___Yes, you are._____ No, you're not. You're in room 202.
Are you a student?	Yes, I am. 2. _____
3. _____	Yes, he is. 4. _____
5. _____	6. _____ No, it's not. It's Mary.

B Pair work. Look at the student web page. Complete the questions and answers. Ask and answer the questions with a partner.

Address: http://www.englishschool.edu/students/sunny.htm

Name: Sun Mi Pak
Nickname: Sunny
Class: English 101, Room 220
Teacher: **Martin Tunick**

My **Favorites**

My favorite athlete: **Ahn Jung Hwan!**
My favorite singer: **Norah Jones**

E-mail me at **sunny@englishschool.edu**

1. ___Is Sun Mi Pak_____ a teacher?
   No, she's not. She's a student.

2. _____ her nickname?
   Yes, _____.

3. Is Ahn Jung Hwan an athlete?
   Yes, _____.

4. Are you in Sunny's class?
   No, _____.

5 Writing

My web page

A Complete the web page with your information.

B Write four or five sentences about yourself. Then read them to the class.

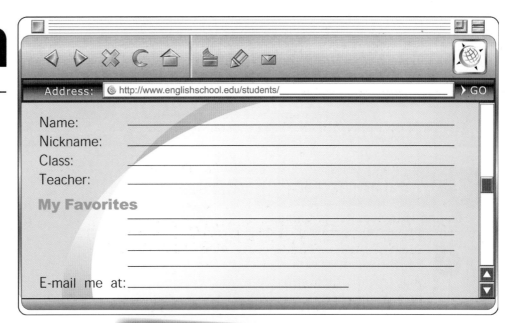

Address: http://www.englishschool.edu/students/_____ ▶ GO

Name: _____
Nickname: _____
Class: _____
Teacher: _____
My Favorites
_____
_____
_____
_____
E-mail me at: _____

6 Communication

My favorites

A Make sentences about your favorites.

| singer | song | actor | movie |

B Choose one of your sentences and write it on a slip of paper. Give it to your teacher.

My favorite actor is Tom Cruise.

My favorite singer is Norah Jones.

C Class activity. Your teacher mixes the slips of paper and gives you a classmate's sentence. Ask your classmates questions. Find the writer of the sentence.

No, he's not.

Is Tom Cruise your favorite actor?

Yes, he is! It's my sentence.

D Repeat the activity with a different sentence.

 Check out the World Link video.   **Practice your English online at** http://elt.thomson.com/worldlink

1 Vocabulary Link

Beijing is the capital of China.

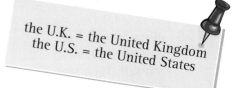

the U.K. = the United Kingdom
the U.S. = the United States

A Say the countries with your teacher. Then write them in the chart.

Brazil
Japan
the U.S.
China
the U.K.
Mexico
Korea
France

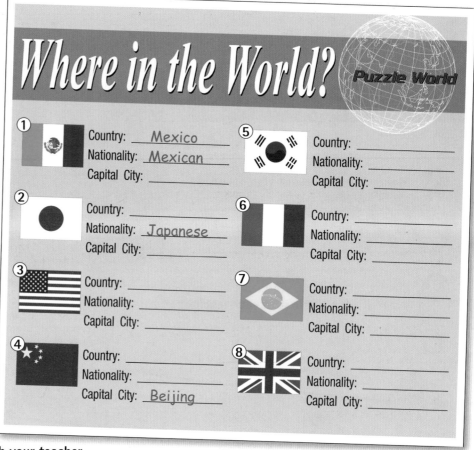

Where in the World? *Puzzle World*

① Country: __Mexico__
Nationality: __Mexican__
Capital City: _____

② Country: _____
Nationality: __Japanese__
Capital City: _____

③ Country: _____
Nationality: _____
Capital City: _____

④ Country: _____
Nationality: _____
Capital City: __Beijing__

⑤ Country: _____
Nationality: _____
Capital City: _____

⑥ Country: _____
Nationality: _____
Capital City: _____

⑦ Country: _____
Nationality: _____
Capital City: _____

⑧ Country: _____
Nationality: _____
Capital City: _____

B Say the nationalities with your teacher.
Then write them in the chart.

Korean   French   American   Brazilian   British   Mexican   Chinese   Japanese

C Say the capital cities with your teacher.
Then write them in the chart.

Beijing   Washington, D.C.   Tokyo   London   Seoul   Mexico City   Paris   Brasilia

D Pair work. Tell your partner about each city.

Beijing is the capital of China.

2 Listening

Are you from Japan?

  A Look at the pictures. Where are the students from?
Listen and write the cities and countries. (CD 1, Track 7)

Ming	Sophia	Marian	Paulo

Country   _China_   _____   _____   _____

City   _____   _Milan_   _____   _____

  B Listen again. Check your answers. (CD 1, Track 8)

C Pair work. Tell your partner about each person.

Ming is from Hong Kong, China.

3 Pronunciation

Stressed syllables

  A Listen and say the countries.
Notice the stressed syllable. (CD 1, Track 9)

CHI na   MEX i co   Co LOM bi a
Bra ZIL   Ko RE a   Cam BO di a

 B Listen and repeat. Circle the stressed syllable. (CD 1, Track 10)

Ca na da   Ja pan   I ta ly
Eng land   Al ge ri a   Ar gen ti na

 C Listen and repeat. Circle the stressed syllable. (CD 1, Track 11)

Spa nish   Ca na di an   I tal ian
A mer i can   Jap a nese   Chi nese

Where are you from?

  A Pair work. **Listen to the conversation. Then practice with a partner.** (CD 1, Track 12)

Carmen: Hi, are you in this class?

Hyun: Yes, I am.

Carmen: Who is the teacher?

Hyun: It's Mr. Allen.

Carmen: Oh. My name is Carmen.

Hyun: I'm Hyun. Where are you from?

Carmen: I'm from Mexico City.
         Where are you from?

Hyun: Seoul, Korea.

B Pair work. **Practice the conversation again with your partner. Use your own information.**

C Class activity. Role play. **Famous people at a party.**

1. **Think of a famous person. Write his or her information below.**

   Name: _____ City and country: _____

2. **Imagine you are the famous person at a party. Meet four more people. Write each person's information.**

> *Hi, I'm Angelina Jolie.*

> *Hi, Angelina. Where are you from?*

Useful Expressions: Asking where someone is from	
Where are you from?	(I'm from) Mexico.
Where is he from?	(He's from) Korea.
Are you from Mexico?	Yes(, I am). No(, I'm not). I'm from Peru.
Which city are you from?	(I'm from) Vancouver.

Name	Where from?
1. Angelina Jolie	Los Angeles, California, the U.S.
2. _____	_____
3. _____	_____
4. _____	_____
5. _____	_____

3. **Tell a partner about the famous people at the party.**

5 Language Link

Question words *who* and *where*

who – asks about people
where – asks about places

who's = who is
where's = where is

A Pair work. **Complete the conversation with *who* or *where*. Then practice with a partner.**

Tammy: Hello?

Arthur: Hello, Tammy?

Tammy: Yes, __who__ is this?

Arthur: It's me, Arthur.

Tammy: Arthur! Hi! _____ are you?

Arthur: I'm in Mexico!

Tammy: In Mexico! _____ in Mexico?

Arthur: In Puerto Vallarta. It's a beautiful city.

Tammy: _____'s with you?

Arthur: I'm here with Tomás. He's from Mexico.

Tammy: Wow, that's great!

B Pair work. **Make four new conversations. Use the words below for the red words in the conversation above. Then, practice with your partner.**

Australia
Sydney
Robert

China
Beijing
Jin

Italy
Rome
Antonio

the U.S.
San Francisco
Martine

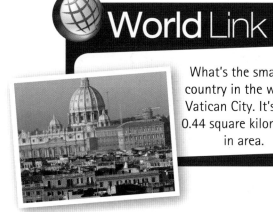

World Link

What's the smallest country in the world? Vatican City. It's only 0.44 square kilometers in area.

C Pair work. Role play. **Imagine you are in another country. Telephone your partner. Where are you? Who is with you? Tell your partner.**

6 Communication

The country and city game

Heads

Tails

Directions:
Play in pairs. Player 1 and player 2 put a marker (an eraser, a coin) on *Start Here*.

1. Player 1 flips two coins:
   - 1 head and 1 tail, move your marker 1 square.
   - 2 tails, move 2 squares.
   - 2 heads, move 3 squares.
2. Player 1 answers the question on the space. For *Free Question*, your partner asks you any question about countries and cities.
3. Then player 2 flips 2 coins, moves, and answers a question.
4. Take turns. You finish at square 24.

20 Mozart was from _____. Name the country.	**21** The capital city of my country is _____.	**22** FREE QUESTION!	**23** Name two states in the United States.	**24 Finish**
19 Where is the Colosseum? Name the city.	**18** Oslo is the capital city of _____	**17** The capital of Greece is _____	**16** FREE QUESTION!	**15** What is the nationality of a person from Colombia?
10 Where is your teacher from?	**11** FREE QUESTION!	**12** David Beckham is from _____. Name the country.	**13** Name two cities in China.	**14** Where is Kuala Lumpur? Name the country.
9 Where does the President of the United States live? Name the city.	**8** Where is the Sydney Opera House? Name the country.	**7** FREE QUESTION!	**6** Where is Antonio Banderas from? Name the country.	**5** What is the capital of Egypt?
Start Here	**1** The capital city of Brazil is _____.	**2** What is the nationality of a person from Spain?	**3** FREE QUESTION!	**4** Where is the Eiffel Tower? Name the city and country.

Answers on page 154.

Countries and Nationalities

Lesson B | What is your city like?

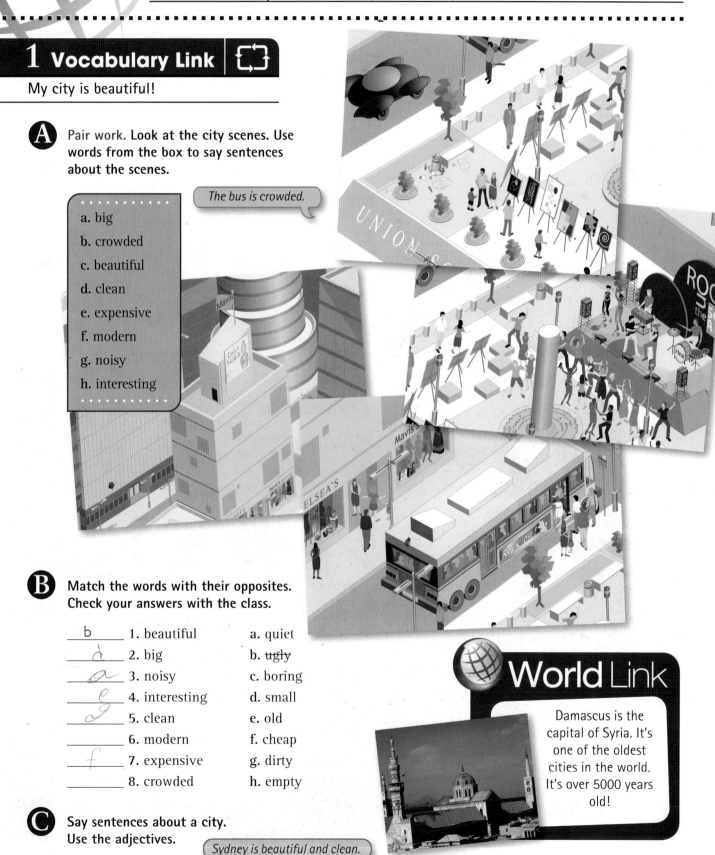

1 Vocabulary Link ⟳

My city is beautiful!

A Pair work. Look at the city scenes. Use words from the box to say sentences about the scenes.

> The bus is crowded.

- a. big
- b. crowded
- c. beautiful
- d. clean
- e. expensive
- f. modern
- g. noisy
- h. interesting

B Match the words with their opposites. Check your answers with the class.

_b_ 1. beautiful	a. quiet	
_d_ 2. big	b. ~~ugly~~	
_a_ 3. noisy	c. boring	
_e_ 4. interesting	d. small	
_g_ 5. clean	e. old	
___ 6. modern	f. cheap	
_f_ 7. expensive	g. dirty	
___ 8. crowded	h. empty	

C Say sentences about a city. Use the adjectives.

> Sydney is beautiful and clean.

World Link

Damascus is the capital of Syria. It's one of the oldest cities in the world. It's over 5000 years old!

What is L.A. like?

A Listen. Complete the sentences. (CD 1, Track 13)

1. Rosa is from _____.
2. Now, she lives in _____.
3. Bill is from _____.
4. Now, he lives in _____.

B Listen. Write adjectives about the cities. (CD 1, Track 14)

1. Los Angeles (L.A.): _not beautiful, interesting_
2. Fortuna: _____
3. New York: _____
4. Miami: _____

Wish you were here...

Golden Gate Bridge

United States of America

Fortuna
San Francisco
Chicago
New York City
Washington D.C.
Los Angeles
Dallas
Miami

* L.A. = Los Angeles

San Fra...
Chinato...

C Listen again and check your answers. (CD 1, Track 15)

3 Reading

A postcard from a friend

In your country, which cities or places are famous or interesting?

A Read the postcard on page 19. Where is Clara?
Check (✓) your answer.

☑ 1. in Chinatown
☐ 2. in a shop
☐ 3. in a café
☐ 4. in a restaurant

ask&
ANSWER
New York is expensive. Is your city expensive?
Name three expensive cities.

B Read the postcard again.

Golden Gate Park
San Francisco, CA

Dear Min,

I'm on vacation in San Francisco. It's beautiful here! Right now, I am in a café in a neighborhood called The Mission. There are many restaurants in this neighborhood. Many people are from Central and South America.

On the front of this postcard is another neighborhood in San Francisco – Chinatown. It's very crowded and interesting. There are many shops and restaurants with food from different parts of China.

I like San Francisco. It's big, but it isn't crowded. Also, it's very clean. The only problem is – it's expensive!

See you soon!
Clara

USA

Yong Min Kim
314 West 36th Street
Apartment 8
New York,
New York 10018

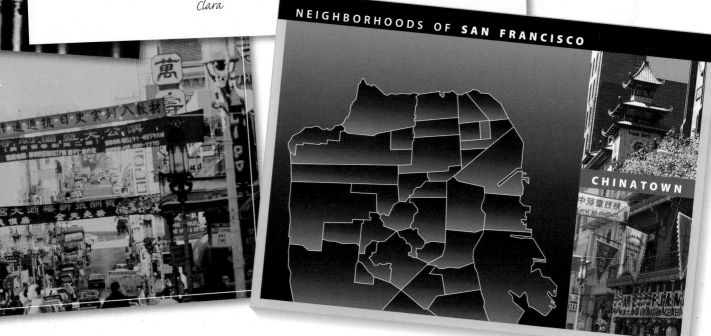

NEIGHBORHOODS OF SAN FRANCISCO

CHINATOWN

C Answer the questions. Circle *True* or *False.*

1. Clara goes to school in San Francisco.   True (False)
2. In The Mission, people are from China.   True   False
3. Chinatown is a crowded neighborhood.   True   False
4. San Francisco is big and clean.   True   False

ask&
ANSWER
What is your city or hometown like?
Name a city you know. What is the city like? What is interesting to see?

4 Language Link

Be + adjective

A Read the sentences. Circle the adjectives.

Tokyo is expensive.   San Francisco isn't crowded.   You aren't Italian.   I am Korean.

B Pair work. Unscramble the questions. Then ask them to a partner.

1. you / Brazilian / are   Are you Brazilian _____ ?
2. the / is / teacher / Australian   _____ ?
3. Mexico City / small / is   _____ ?
4. modern / New York City / is   _____ ?
5. city / your / is / polluted   _____ ?

C Read each pair of sentences. Then make one sentence using *and*.

1. Paris is old. Paris is beautiful.   Paris is old and beautiful _____ .
2. Chinatown is busy. It is interesting. Chinatown is busy and interesting _____ .
3. Eva is half Italian. She is half Irish. _____ .
4. London is expensive. It is busy.   _____ .
5. Seoul is big. It's modern.   _____ .
6. My town is small. It is boring.   _____ .

5 Writing

A postcard from my city

ten million= 10,000,000

A On a piece of paper, write a postcard to Clara. Tell her about your city.

Dear Clara,

Hi! My name is Eun Mi. I'm a student. I'm from Seoul, Korea. Seoul is very big! Ten million people live here. I'm in a café on a famous street — Insadong. This neighborhood is interesting. There are art galleries and tea houses. What is your city like? Write back soon.

Eun Mi

Clara
214 W
Apt. 1
1001

Seoul, Korea

B Pair work. Exchange postcards with a partner. Ask two or three questions about your partner's postcard.

6 Communication

Vacation!

 A Look at the photos. Read the answers below. Then write the questions.

Venice

_____ Venice?

Venice is in Italy.

_____ like?

Venice is very old and beautiful. The city is interesting. It's a great place for vacation!

B Where is a good place for vacation?
Write your ideas in the chart.

	My idea	My partner's idea
Place		
Where is it?		
What is it like?		

C Pair work. Interview your partner. Complete the chart with his or her ideas.

D Choose one place for vacation. Tell the class your choice.

 Check out the World Link video.

 Practice your English online at http://elt.thomson.com/worldlink

Interesting Products

Lesson A | Personal items

1 Vocabulary Link

What's this?

A Match the words with items in Paula's room.

1. ~~laptop (computer)~~
2. watch
3. cell phone
4. purse
5. key
6. camera
7. answering machine
8. CD player

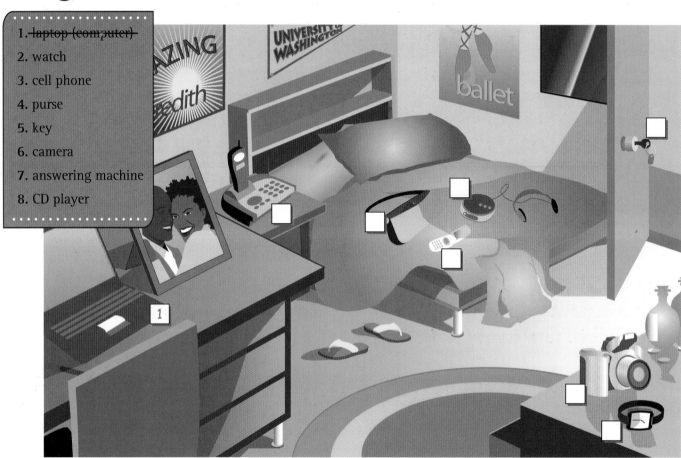

B Write *a* or *an* next to each item.

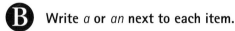

1. _____ laptop
2. _____ watch
3. _____ cell phone
4. _____ purse
5. _____ key
6. _____ camera
7. _____ answering machine
8. _____ CD player

a + consonant sound
an + vowel sound

C Pair work. Point to each thing in the room above. Ask and answer the question "What's this?"

What's this?

It's a laptop.

2 Listening

A birthday gift

 A Listen.
Number the gifts 1 to 4. One gift is extra.
(CD 1, Track 16)

B Listen again.
Circle the gift for Tony.
(CD 1, Track 17)

C Pair work.
What is your favorite gift? Tell a classmate.

Planet Electronics
Year End Super Sale

*Great Gift Ideas!

Digital Camera $500
- 4.0 Megapixel
- High Quality Lens

On Sale! **NOW $25**
CD Player $~~~~
- Playback Mode
- Remote Control

Blank CDs From $10
- Various Makers
- 700 MB
- 20, 40 & 60 Packs

Watch $100
- Silver Finish
- Time & Date

Best Buy! **Cell Phone** $99
- Auto Roaming
- Long Battery Life

3 Pronunciation

Linking with *n*

 A Listen and repeat. Notice how the *n* sound links to the start of the next word. (CD 1, Track 18)

What's this?	It's an umbrella.	[n + vowel]
Who is the teacher?	John is.	[n + vowel]
What are these?	They're brand-new pencils.	[n + n sound]

B Listen and repeat.
Link [‿] the *n* sound to the start of the next word. (CD 1, Track 19)

1. Who's that?   He's an actor.
2. Who are they?   Ben and Mary are my friends.
3. Is this her CD player?   No, Jan never listens to music.
4. What's this?   It's an ID card.
5. Is she a student?   No, Joan isn't a student.

C Pair work. Ask and answer the questions in B with a partner.

World Link

Roses are a popular gift. However, different colors have different meanings. Red usually means "love," yellow means "friendship," and pink can say "thank you!"

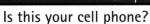

Is this your cell phone?

A   Group work. **Listen to the conversation. Then practice with two partners.**
(CD 1, Track 20)

Paula: Alison, is this your cell phone?

Alison: No, it's not. Ask that man.

Paula: Excuse me!

Man: Yes?

Paula: Is this your cell phone?

Man: Yes, it is! Thank you so much!

Paula: Sure, no problem.

B Write *a* or *an* next to each word.

1. ___a___ notebook

2. _____ pen

3. _____ address book

4. _____ backpack

5. _____ umbrella

6. _____ pencil

C Class activity. Role play. Lost items

1. Imagine you lost one of the items in **B**. Write the name of the item on a piece of paper. Draw a small picture. Give the paper to your teacher.

an address book

2. Your teacher mixes the papers and gives one to everyone in the class.

3. Find the owner of the lost item.

Excuse me. Is this your address book?

No, it's not.

Yes, it is! Thanks a lot!

Useful Expressions:	
Saying *Thank You*	Replies
Thank you so much.	You're welcome.
Thank you.	My pleasure.
Thanks a lot.	Sure, no problem.
Thanks.	

5 Language Link

Plurals; *this/that/these/those*

they're = they are

 A Read the questions and answers in the chart.
Say them with your teacher.

Singular nouns	Plural nouns
What's this? / What's that?	What are these? / What are those?
It's . . . an answering machine. a dictionary. a watch. a glass. a dish.	They're . . . answering machines. dictionaries. watches. glasses. dishes.

B Make each noun plural. Pay attention to spelling.

1. umbrella ___umbrellas___
2. city _____
3. class _____

4. country _____
5. beach _____
6. purse _____

7. brush _____
8. camera _____
9. ID card _____

C Complete the questions with *this*, *that*, *these*, or *those*.
Then write the answers.

Use *this* and *these* for things near you.

Use *that* and *those* for things away from you.

1. What's ___this_____?
   It's ___an answering machine___.

2. What are _____?
   They're _____.

3. What are _____?
   They're _____.

4. What's _____?
   It's _____.

 D Pair work. Check your answers with a partner.

Thanks a lot!

 A Pair work. Practice the conversation with a partner. Then practice again with a different gift idea.

> Tony: Oh, let's see . . . What's this?
> Wow, a CD player!
> Thanks a lot, Paula!
>
> Paula: Sure, Tony. I'm glad you like it.

 B Think of a gift. Write the name of the gift on a small piece of paper. Fold the paper in half.

sunglasses

a watch

 C Class activity. Gift giving
1. Exchange gifts with a partner. Thank your partner. Write the name of the gift in the chart below.
2. Exchange the gift you got with a new partner. Do this four times. Write each new gift in the chart.

Gifts

D Pair work. What's your favorite gift? Tell your partner.

What's your favorite gift?

The sunglasses.

Interesting Products

Lesson B | Modern electronics

1 Vocabulary Link

Electronic items

A Match the words with the electronic items in the pictures. Write the numbers. Then practice saying the words.

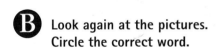

1. camcorder
2. stereo
3. TV
4. MP3 player
5. DVD player
6. VCR

B Look again at the pictures. Circle the correct word.

1. The camcorder is expensive / inexpensive.
2. The large-screen TV is heavy / light.
3. The MP3 player is small / large.
4. The TV is new / old.

C Pair work. Complete the chart with the adjectives in B. Check your answers with a partner.

Age	Size	Weight	Cost
old	large		

2 Listening

Is this your new DVD player?

  A Listen. Number the pictures (1, 2, 3) in the order you hear. (CD 1, Track 21)

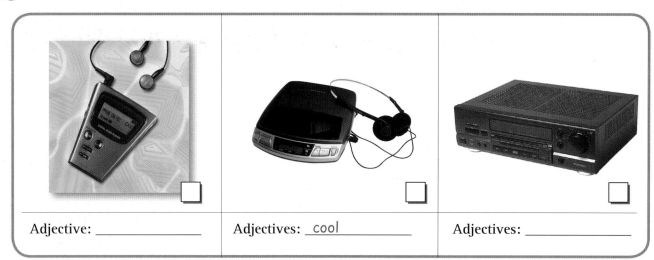

| Adjective: _____ | Adjectives: _cool_____ | Adjectives: _____ |

 B Listen again. What adjectives describe each item?
Write the adjectives on the chart above. (CD 1, Track 22)

3 Reading

Electronics for sale

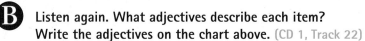

Do you buy electronics on the Internet?

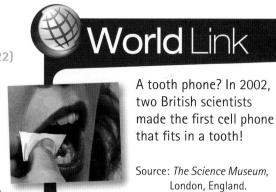

World Link

A tooth phone? In 2002, two British scientists made the first cell phone that fits in a tooth!

Source: *The Science Museum,* London, England.

 A Pair work. Circle the electronic items you have. Describe them to a partner.

I have a CD player. It's small and . . .

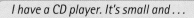   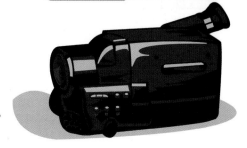

B Look at the web page on page 29. Which product is excellent?
Which product is terrible?

28 Unit 3 • Interesting Products

Read people's opinions about these electronic products.

Address: http://www.bestrating.com/d_gadgets/funplayers.htm ❯ GO

| HOME | FASHION | HOME APPLIANCES | COMPUTERS | BOOKS | MUSIC | DIGITAL GADGETS |

{ *Digital Gadgets* }·········· **BestRating**
before you buy

iListen MP3 Player   Rating: ★ ★ ★ ★ ★

iListen is a small and lightweight MP3 player. Headphones are included. It's on sale now for $99. It's a very cool, inexpensive player!

Sonic CD Player   Rating: ★ ★ ★ ★ ★

This inexpensive, portable CD player is a new product from Sonic. It's a big, heavy machine, and the audio is terrible! A radio and headphones are included.

PVC Camcorder   Rating: ★ ★ ★ ★ ★

This is a new product from PVC electronics. This small and lightweight camcorder is also a camera and an audio player. It's an expensive product.

Danson DVD Player   Rating: ★ ★ ★ ★ ★

This DVD player plays DVDs, CD videos, and audio CDs. It's a small, inexpensive player. Buy it now and get a free DVD movie!

Rating: 1 - 5 stars

★ ★ ★ ★ ★ = Terrible
★ ★ ★ ★ ★ = Bad
★ ★ ★ ★ ★ = OK
★ ★ ★ ★ ★ = Good
★ ★ ★ ★ ★ = Excellent

 Complete the chart with information from the reading.

Product	Rating	Reason
1. MP3 player	It's excellent.	It's small and lightweight.
2. CD player	It's terrible.	
3.		
4. DVD player		

ask**&**
ANSWER

Think of an electronics company.
Name two of their products, describe them, and give them a rating.

4 Language Link

Adjectives and nouns

Adjectives describe nouns.
Paris is beautiful.
noun   adjective

A Read the sentences. Circle the adjectives. Underline the nouns.

1. Your camera is (nice.)
2. Those are beautiful sunglasses.
3. This is a Swiss watch.
4. My books are new.

B Write the sentences from **A** in the chart.

	Be + adjective	Adjective + noun
singular	This phone is expensive. _____.	This is an expensive phone. _____.
plural	These phones are expensive. _____.	These are expensive phones. _____.

C Complete the sentences with *a*, *an*, or nothing.

1. That's ___a___ nice laptop.
2. This is _____ inexpensive CD player.
3. These are _____ expensive glasses.
4. What are those? They're _____ new dictionaries.
5. Is this _____ old TV? Yes, it is.

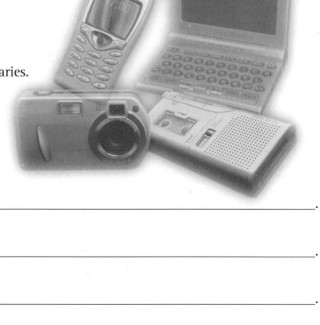

D Unscramble the sentences.

1. (is / a / This / DVD player / terrible)
   <u>This is a terrible DVD player</u>   .
2. (MP3 player / An / gift / nice / is / a)
   _____ .
3. (are / These / camcorders / Japanese)
   _____ .
4. (inexpensive / are / They / cameras)
   _____ .
5. (an / is / interesting / This / book)
   _____ .

5 Writing

My product rating

A Think of a product. Complete the chart. Write three or four sentences about it on a separate piece of paper.

Name of product: _____
Where from: _____
Rating: _____
Reason: _____

Name: iListen MP3 player
Where from: the U.S.
Rating: ★ ★ ★ ★ ★
Reason: iListen is a small and lightweight MP3 player.
It's from the U.S.
It's a cool, inexpensive player!

B Pair work. Read your partner's sentences. Do you know the product? Is the information correct?

6 Communication

Our favorite products

A Look at the picture. Write adjectives to describe the product. Write two sentences about it.

IBC Laptop
Now On Sale!
1.5 lb / 0.68 kg

adjectives:

_____
_____

sentences:

1. _____
2. _____

B On a separate piece of paper, draw a picture of a real or imaginary product. Write the name of the product. Write two or three sentences about it.

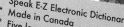
* Speak E-Z Electronic Dictionary
* Made in Canada
* Five languages! English, Japanese, Korean, Mandarin, Spanish
* Audio for pronunciation

C Class activity. Share your product with the class. What product is your favorite?

 Check out the World Link video.　 **Practice your English online at** http://elt.thomson.com/worldlink

1 Storyboard

A Pair work. Adriano and Li Mei are students. It's the first day of class. Complete the conversations.

B Group work. In groups of three, practice the conversations.

C Group work. Switch roles and practice the conversations again.

2 See it and say it

 A Pair work. **Work with a partner. Quickly find these things in the picture. Ask and answer the questions** *What's this?* or *What are these?*

> *What's this?*

> cell phone   watch   backpack   keys   camera   sunglasses

> *It's a cell phone.*

B Pair work. **Talk about the picture with a partner.**

- Where are the people now?
- Where are they from?

- Who is on vacation? Who isn't?
- Ask one more question about the picture.

C Pair work. **Choose one pair of people. Role-play a short conversation between the people.**

> *Hello. I'm Fernando.*

> *Hi, Fernando.*

3 Countries and nationalities

Read the clues. Complete the crossword puzzle.
Check your answers with a partner.

Across

1. The capital of _____ is Berlin.
4. Beijing is the capital of _____.
6. The Queen of England lives in this city.
7. A person from Brazil is _____.
9. The capital of Canada is _____.
10. The _____ Opera House is in Australia.

Down

2. In this country, people speak Spanish.
3. Tokyo is the capital of _____.
5. _____ is the capital of Korea.
7. A person from the U.K. is _____.
8. This city is the capital of Italy.

4 What's this?

Pair work. Choose five words from the box.
Draw a picture of each word. Your partner guesses the words.

laptop	cell phone	purse	keys	sunglasses
camera	umbrella	watch	wallet	notebooks
pen	dictionary	backpack	ID card	pencils
address book	CD player	stereo	TV	VCR

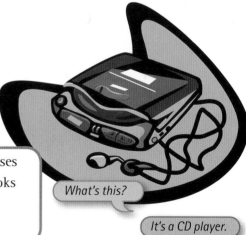

What's this?

It's a CD player.

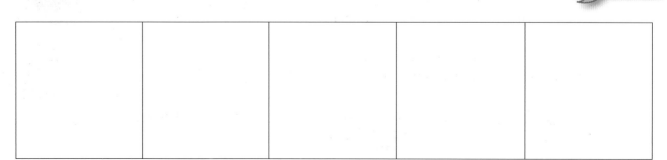

5 Listening: 20 Questions

A Listen. These people are playing a game.
Complete the information about the person. (CD 1 Track 23)

Male _____   Female _____   Job: _____
Nationality: _____   Nickname: _____

B Listen again. Look at the information in A.
Circle the correct picture below. (CD 1 Track 24)

Jennifer Aniston

Justin Timberlake

Angelina Jolie

Jennifer Lopez

C Pair work. Think of a famous person. Your partner asks you *yes/no* questions to guess the person.

Is it a man?

No, it's a woman.

Is she from the United States?

Yes, she is.

6 Small town, big city

A Study the picture. Look at the words in the box.
What words go with the picture? Circle them.

small	boring	dirty
clean	expensive	big
safe	old	noisy
modern	quiet	interesting

B Pair work. Use the words in the box to talk
about the picture. Take turns with a partner.

C Pair work. Tell your partner about a famous
town or city. Your partner guesses the city.

*This city is very old. It's a
big city. It's in England.*

Is it London?

1 Vocabulary Link

Things we do

A What are these people doing? Match each activity with a person.

1. listening to music
2. studying
3. eating
4. exercising
5. sleeping
6. cooking
7. watching TV
8. singing
9. reading
10. playing the guitar

Pamela [2]

Sophia [1]

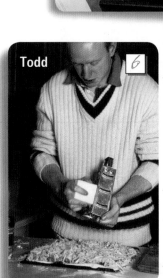

Todd [6]

Julie [8]

Tina [9]

Bill [10]

Klaus [4]

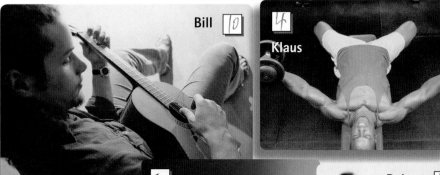

Kate [5]

Robert [7]

Andrea [3]

B Pair work. Ask and answer questions about the pictures with a partner.

What is Todd doing?

He's cooking.

2 Listening

What are you doing?

 A Listen to the conversations. Number the pictures in the order that you hear. (CD 1, Track 25)

 B Listen again. Who is doing each activity? Check (✓) all the possible answers. (CD 1, Track 26)

	Selena	John			Julie	Ed			Alex	Lori
a. studying	✓	☐	**a.** cooking dinner		☐	☐	**a.** listening to music		☐	☐
b. e-mailing a friend	☐	☐	**b.** e-mailing a friend		☐	☐	**b.** watching TV		☐	☐
c. reading a book	☐	☐	**c.** studying		☐	☐	**c.** playing the guitar		☐	☐

C Pair work. Tell your partner about each person in B.

Selena is studying.

3 Pronunciation

Question intonation

 A Listen to these questions. Say them with your teacher. (CD 1, Track 27)

Yes/No questions	Wh- questions
Are you cooking? [↗]	What are you doing? [↘]
Is he listening to music? [↗]	How is she doing? [↘]

 B Pair work. Listen to the questions. Write [↗] or [↘]. Practice with a partner. (CD 1, Track 28)

1. Who's singing? [↘]
2. How are you doing? [ ]
3. Are they playing basketball? [ ]
4. What book are you reading? [ ]
5. Is Mary talking on the phone? [ ]
6. What are Carmen and Tim cooking? [ ]

A Pair work. **Listen to the conversation. Then practice with a partner.** (CD 1, Track 29)

Shinja:	Hello?
Luis:	Hey, Shinja. It's Luis.
Shinja:	Hi, Luis. How are you doing?
Luis:	Great! How about you?
Shinja:	I'm okay. What are you doing?
Luis:	I'm studying for a test. What are you doing?
Shinja:	I'm watching a great video. Too bad you're studying.

In spoken English, "How are you doing?" is often said, "How're ya doin'?"

B Pair work. **Make four new conversations. Use the words below for the red words in the conversation above. Practice with a partner.**

1. Larry / so-so / writing a paper
2. Cathy / all right / cooking
3. Michael / all right / cleaning the apartment
4. Wendy / okay / exercising

 C Class activity. **Role play. Telephone three people in your class. Use the conversation above and the Useful Expressions. Complete the chart below.**

Useful Expressions: Asking how someone is (1)		
How are you doing?	(I'm) fine. all right. okay. so-so.	How about you?

Name	How is the person?	What is he or she doing?
Shinja	She's okay.	She's watching a video.
.		

D Class activity. **Tell the class about the people on the chart.**

Max is doing fine. He's cooking dinner.

5 Language Link

The present continuous

A Write the sentences in the chart.

Use contractions in speaking.
I am reading. = I'm reading.
I am not studying. = I'm not studying.

> ~~She is exercising.~~   No, he's not.
> Yes, they are.   They are studying.

Wh– questions	Positive answers	Negative answers
What are you doing? What is Anna doing? What are Jo and Amy doing?	I am reading. 1. ___She is exercising___. 2. _____.	I am not studying. She is not reading. They are not exercising.

Yes/No questions	Positive answers	Negative answers
Are you watching TV? Is John studying? Are Tim and Sam playing Frisbee?	Yes, I am. Yes, he is. 4. _____.	No, I'm not. 3. _____. No, they're not.

B Complete the sentences with the present continuous. Pay attention to spelling.

Spelling Rules

cook	cooking
study	studying
exercise	exercising
shop	shopping
jog	jogging

1. Kelly (read) _____is reading_____ a book.
2. I (cook) _____ dinner for my friends.
3. They (study) _____ for a test.
4. Tom (not / exercise) _____ right now.
5. Mario and I (not / sit) _____ on the floor.
6. You and Bill (use) _____ the computers.

C Pair work. Complete the telephone conversation. Use the correct form of the verb. Practice with a partner.

A: Hello?
B: Hi, Mark. It's Tina.
   What (you / do) ___are you doing?___ ?
A: I (read) _____.
B: What (you / read) _____?
A: The book is called *The Joy Luck Club*. It's by Amy Tan.
   (you / study) _____ for a test?
B: No, I (be) _____. I (listen to music) _____.

World Link

Japanese people spend the most money on books every year — $182 (U.S.) for EVERY person in Japan!

Source: *The Economist Pocket World in Figures, 2003*

Lesson A • Everyday activities   **39**

6 Communication

What are they doing?

A What are the people doing? Match each activity with a picture.

1. ~~talking on the phone~~   4. drinking
2. arguing   5. laughing
3. drawing   6. dancing

B Pair work. Look at the two pictures. With a partner, find the differences.

> In picture A, a man is playing the guitar. In picture B, he isn't playing the guitar. He's . . .

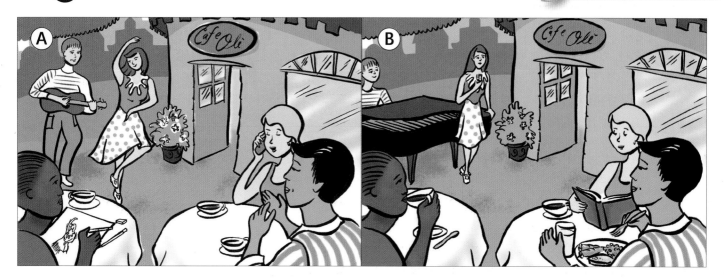

Activities and Interests

Lesson B | At school

1 Vocabulary Link

School subjects

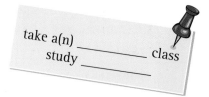

take a(n) _____ class
study _____

A Match the subjects with the books. Add two more subjects.

1. ~~writing~~
2. math
3. science
4. music
5. literature
6. English
7. art
8. business
9. cooking
10. history
11. _____
12. _____

B Pair work. What are your favorite subjects? Tell your partner.

> *My favorite subject is music.*

> *My favorite subjects are English and art.*

2 Listening

I'm taking a math class.

 A Listen. Check (✓) the classes Brandon and Sheila are taking. (CD 1, Track 30)

	art history	yoga	English	math	science	writing	business
Brandon	☐	☐	☐	☐	☐	☐	☐
Sheila	☐	☐	☐	☐	☐	☐	☐

 B Pair work. Listen again. Complete the sentences. Check your answers with a partner. (CD 1, Track 31)

1. Sheila is taking 3 / 4 / 5 classes.
2. Brandon is taking 3 / 4 / 5 classes.
3. Brandon and Sheila are both taking one class on the _____.

3 Reading

What are you studying?

Years in high school or university in the U.S.

freshman = 1st year
sophomore = 2nd year
junior = 3rd year
senior = 4th year

A Pair work. Fill in the blanks with information about yourself or someone you know. Share the information with a partner.

Name: _____

University: _____

Year in university: *freshman*   *sophomore*   *junior*   *senior*

Major (circle one): *art*   *business*   *computer science*

English   *engineering*   *history*   *math*   *other* _____

> *My boyfriend is a sophomore at the University of Washington. His major is computer science.*

B Read the interview.

School Buzz: What are you studying?

In this issue of *Student Life*, Sandra Moore is talking to students at the University of Chicago.

Sandra: Derek Anderson is eating lunch at the cafeteria today. Thanks for talking with me, Derek.

Derek: Sure. No problem.

Sandra: Please tell our readers a little about yourself.

Derek: Well, I'm from Toronto, Canada. I'm a junior, and I'm majoring in business.

Sandra: Which classes are you taking?

Derek: This semester, I'm taking three business classes, a writing class, and a Portuguese class.

Sandra: That's interesting. Why are you studying Portuguese?

Derek: Well, my girlfriend is from Brazil.

Sandra: *(laughing)* Oh, I see! So how are you doing in your classes?

Derek: I'm doing very well in my business classes. I'm getting As. I'm not doing so well in writing.

Sandra: What about the Portuguese class?

Derek: I'm doing okay. I practice with my girlfriend.

Sandra: That's great! Thanks again for your time.

C Complete Sandra's notes about the interview.

Name: _____
Where from: _____
Classes this semester: _____
_____
_____

How is he or she doing in the classes?
He's doing well in business class.
But he's not _____
_____
_____

D Pair work. **Discuss the questions with a partner.**

1. What classes are you taking?
   _____
   _____

2. How are you doing in your classes?
   ___ well
   ___ okay
   ___ not so well
   ___ terribly

3. Why are you studying English?
   ___ for fun
   ___ for travel
   ___ for my major
   ___ for my job
   ___ to go to college
   ___ other _____

World Link

60% of American college students change their major more than once.

The present continuous: extended time

Joan is studying Spanish.

Joan is studying Spanish this month.

 A Look at the two sentences.
How are they similar?
How are they different?

 B Write the sentences below
in the correct place in the chart.

~~I'm studying for a test right now.~~	~~I'm taking three business classes this semester.~~
Craig is talking on the phone.	Simone is sitting on the floor.
Maria is majoring in English.	Daisuke isn't doing well in his Spanish class.

actions happening *right now*

I'm studying for a test right now_____.
_____.
_____.

actions happening *these days*

I'm taking three business classes this semester_.
_____.
_____.

 C Complete the sentences.
Use the present continuous.

☑ How are you?

To: sean@worldlink.com   **Date:** October 10
From: eric@worldlink.com   **Subject:** How are you?

Hey Sean,

How are you? Well, here I am at the University of Chicago as a freshman! It's great! **1.** (I / e-mail)
_____ you from my room. **2.** (I / use) _____ my new laptop. **3.** This
semester (I / take) _____ five classes—two writing classes, two business classes, and
a Spanish class. **4.** The classes are interesting and (I / learn) _____ a lot. The teachers
are very good. **5.** (I / live) _____ in the dorms. **6.** (I / meet) _____ a lot of
new people. The students here are nice. My roommate is Yong Gu, a guy from Korea.
7. (He / teach) _____ me to speak Korean.

Write soon,

Eric

D Look at the sentences in C.

1. Which sentences are about actions happening right now? Circle the numbers.

2. Which are about actions happening these days? Underline the numbers.

5 Writing

A student interview

A Pair work. Interview your partner. Use the questions below and some of your own.

1. What classes are you taking these days?
2. How are you doing in the classes?
3. What are your favorite subjects?

B On a separate piece of paper, write about your partner.

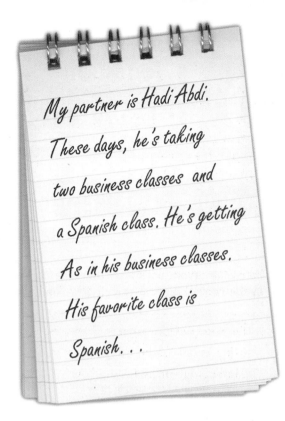

My partner is Hadi Abdi. These days, he's taking two business classes and a Spanish class. He's getting As in his business classes. His favorite class is Spanish...

6 Communication

Two truths and a lie

A Think of things you are doing these days. Write some ideas below.

These days, I'm . . .

majoring in _____.

studying _____.

taking a _____ class.

learning to _____.

living _____.

doing well in _____.

other: _____.

B Write two true ideas and one lie about things you are doing these days.

Truth	_____
Truth	_____
Lie	_____

C Group work. Get into a group of 3 or 4 people. Read your sentences to the group. Your partners ask you questions. They guess the lie.

I'm taking a French class.

Really? Where?

Why are you studying French?

 Check out the World Link video.

 Practice your English online at http://elt.thomson.com/worldlink

5 Food

Lesson A | Food and eating habits

1 Vocabulary Link

What's on the menu?

 A Pair work. Work with a partner. Match the food on the menu with the pictures. Write the numbers in the circles. Some words have no picture.

Dee Dee's Diner

Breakfast

| 1 | Cereal | $1.50 |
| 2 | Bacon & Eggs | $2.95 |

Lunch & Dinner

3	Soup & Salad	$5.75
4	Chicken Sandwich	$4.75
5	Pizza	$7.00
6	Fish	$8.95
7	Chicken	$7.95
8	Steak	$9.95
9	Pasta with Tomato Sauce	$6.95

Drinks

10	Coffee	$1.25
11	Tea	$1.25
12	Soda	$1.25
13	Bottled Water	$1.00

Desserts

| 14 | Chocolate Cake | $2.25 |
| 15 | Ice Cream | $2.00 |

B Pair work. With your partner, think of other things you could add to the menu for each section.

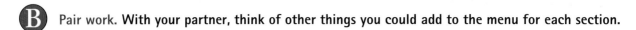

C Pair work. What are your favorite foods and drinks? Tell your partner.

I like fried rice and tea . . .

to make dinner = to cook dinner
to have dinner = to eat dinner

2 Listening

I'm making dinner.

 A **Listen. Number the pictures in the order that you hear.** (CD 1, Track 32)

 B **Listen again. Check (✓) the foods or drinks each person talks about.** (CD 1, Track 33)

	cake	soup	tea	salad	bottled water	chicken
Lance	☐	☐	☐	☐	☐	☐
Cami	☐	☐	☐	☐	☐	☐
Mark	☐	☐	☐	☐	☐	☐

ask&
ANSWER
What do you have for breakfast, lunch, and dinner?

3 Pronunciation

And

 A **Listen and repeat. Notice the *and* sound.** (CD 1, Track 34)

Diet? Never! Britney
Spears' favorite foods
include ice cream,
pasta, and hot dogs!

Written	Spoken
cream and sugar	cream 'n' sugar
salt and pepper	salt 'n' pepper
bread and butter	bread 'n' butter

B **Practice saying these sentences with reduced *and*.**
Then listen and repeat. (CD 1, Track 35)

1. A soup and salad, please.
2. I like toast and butter with my bacon and eggs.
3. I like Mexican and Japanese food.
4. In Korea, many people eat kimchi and rice for breakfast.
5. Simon and Grace want cake and a cup of coffee for dessert.

Lesson A • Food and eating habits 47

4 Speaking

Do you like Italian food?

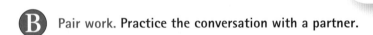

A Listen to the conversation.
Does Jason like all Italian food? (CD 1, Track 36)

Jason: Hey, Marnie, I'm hungry. Let's eat.

Marnie: Okay. Do you like Italian food?

Jason: Yes, I love it!

Marnie: I know a great restaurant. It's called La Cucina. Their fish is delicious.

Jason: Oh, I don't really like fish.

Marnie: Well, they have pasta and pizza, too.

Jason: Sounds good—I love pizza. Let's go!

Restaurant name: Applebee's
Kind of food: American
Food on the menu: soup, sandwiches, hamburgers, pasta

B Pair work. Practice the conversation with a partner.

C 1. Think of two restaurants. Write the information.

Restaurant name: _____   Restaurant name: _____

Kind of food: _____   Kind of food: _____

Food on the menu: _____   Food on the menu: _____

_____   _____

2. Pair work. Make new conversations with your partner. Use the conversation in A and the Useful Expressions.

Hey Pablo, I'm hungry. Let's eat dinner.

Useful Expressions: Talking about likes and dislikes		
Do you like Italian food?	Yes! I love it!	☺
Do you like fish?	Yes, I like it a lot.	☺
	Yes, it's okay.	😐
	No, I don't really like it.	☹
	No, I can't stand it.	☹

Okay. Do you like Chinese food?

ask&
ANSWER

What is your favorite restaurant or place to eat?
What foods from other countries do you know?
Which ones do you like? Which ones do you not like?

5 Language Link

The simple present

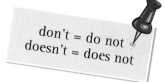

don't = do not
doesn't = does not

A Study the chart. Notice the verbs.

I			He		
You	speak	English.	He	speaks	English.
We	don't speak		She	doesn't speak	
They					

B Complete Tomoko's schedule with a verb.
Then, complete your schedule.

have   has   speak   speaks   do   does   go   goes

Tomoko's schedule

She __has__ eggs for breakfast.
She _____ to school at 7:30.
She _____ Japanese and English at school.
She _____ her homework in the library.

My schedule

I _____ _____ for breakfast.
I _____ to school at _____.
I _____ _____ at school.
I _____ my homework _____.

C Now write sentences using *don't* or *doesn't*. Use the verbs in B.

Tomoko's schedule

She _doesn't_ _have_ cereal for breakfast.
She _____ _____ to school at 8:30.
She _____ _____ French at school.
She _____ _____ her homework in class.

My schedule

I _____ _____ _____ for breakfast.
I _____ _____ to school at _____.
I _____ _____ _____ at school.
I _____ _____ my homework _____.

D Complete the sentences. Use the simple present.
Pay attention to spelling.

1. Jane (like) __likes__ chicken and fish. She (not / like) _____ steak.

2. I (not / eat) _____ meat. I'm a vegetarian.

3. Duncan (study) _____ at the library. We (not / study) _____ at the library.

4. Naoki (have) _____ tea for breakfast.

5. Jo and Marc (do) _____ their homework together. Li (not / do) _____ his homework with them.

A You are having a dinner party.
Read about your six dinner guests.

Mary Summerset

She's from London. She likes
music. She doesn't eat much meat.
She is Min Chul's girlfriend.

William March

He's from Canada. He speaks
Portuguese and English. He loves
spicy food. He plays soccer.

Lisa Leung

She's from Hong Kong.
She's an actress. She speaks
English, Spanish, and Chinese.
She doesn't drink alcohol.

Paula Marques

She's from São Paulo, Brazil.
She studies art at the University
of London in England.
She likes soccer.

Min Chul Kim

He's from Pusan, Korea.
He's an actor in London.
He likes drawing.
He loves Italian food.

Diego Flores

He's from Buenos Aires,
Argentina. He lives in Canada
now. He teaches music at the
University of Toronto.

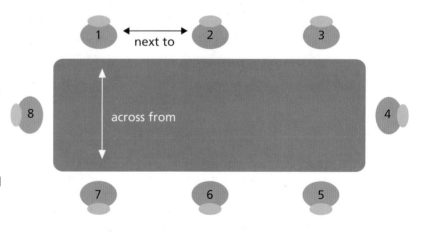

 B Pair work. **Plan the party!**
1. With a partner, make a menu
   for the dinner party.
   Think about your dinner guests'
   likes and dislikes.
2. Choose a seat at the table for
   each person. Include yourself and
   your partner.

 C Pair work. **Get together with a new partner. Explain your menu and table seating.**

> *Here's our menu. For
> dinner, we are having . . .*

> *Paula is in seat one. She's sitting next to William.
> They both like soccer. They're a good pair.*

Food

1 Vocabulary Link

Food festivals

 A   Look at the pictures. Read about these festivals.
Notice the words in red.

Boston, Massachusetts U.S.A.   **Travel Tips: Card #14**

Every year, the city of Boston, in the U.S.,
has an Italian festival. It's in the summer.
Many people visit Boston then.

★ Be sure to try the
delicious pasta
dishes. For dessert,
have some *gelato*,
(Italian ice cream)!

Washington, D.C. U.S.A.   **Travel Tips: Card #26**

Every year in Washington, D.C., there is a special
Japanese festival. There is a big parade. Some
people wear traditional Japanese clothes.

 ★ There are many foods
to try — including
Japanese noodles
and sushi.

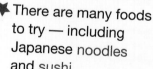

B   Pair work. Discuss the questions with a partner.

1. Do you ever eat pasta dishes, noodles, or sushi?
2. What is your favorite kind of ice cream?
3. Name a festival you know. What do people eat? What do they drink?
4. Do you like parades? On what days are there parades?
5. Look at the picture of the Japanese festival in A. The people are wearing traditional
   Japanese clothes called *kimono*. Do you ever wear traditional clothes?

A Look at the recipe.
Match each picture with a food.

a

b

c

d

Angelina's Pasta with Sauce

tomatoes __a__   garlic _____

onion _____   ground meat

pasta   oil   sausage _____

Cook garlic and onions. Add tomatoes.

Cook ten minutes. Add meat and

sausage. Cook for one hour. Cook

pasta. Add tomato sauce to pasta.

 B Listen. What foods are the people making?
Number them in the order that you hear.
(CD 1, Track 37)

World Link

In Australia, the #1 topping for pizza is eggs. In Chile, it's mussels and clams. In the U.S., pepperoni is the favorite.

mole sauce

shepherd's pie

gyro

- [ ] Mexico
- [ ] Spain

- [ ] Ireland only
- [ ] The U.K and Ireland

- [ ] Italy
- [ ] Greece

 C Listen again. Where are the foods from? Check (✓) the country. (CD 1, Track 38)

3 Reading

What's your favorite food festival?

> Are there food festivals in your country?

A Look quickly at the reading. Match a picture with a festival.

B Read about these food festivals.

Fabulous Festivals!

Do you like food? Well, you'll love these International Food Festivals.

a. Do you know the Gilroy Garlic Festival? It is in the small town of Gilroy, California, near San Francisco. The festival is for three days in July. More than 100,000 people visit the festival. They have food and drink, all made using garlic—bread, pizza, beer, even ice cream! Some people wear clothes made of garlic. It's great fun!

b. In the city of Phuket, Thailand, the Chinese community has a vegetarian festival every year in the fall. For ten days, people don't eat meat or drink alcohol. There are many delicious vegetarian dishes to eat. Many people wear white. Also, there are interesting shows. Some men eat fire and walk on hot coals!

c. The Oktoberfest in Munich, Germany, is a lot of fun. People from all over the world visit Germany at the end of September. The festival lasts for sixteen days. People drink delicious German beer and eat chicken and sausages. There are also parades and traditional German music.

C Make the sentences true.

1. The garlic festival is in ~~San Francisco~~. ___Gilroy___
2. At the Oktoberfest, people drink soda. _____
3. The Thai festival is for 16 days. _____
4. The Oktoberfest is in Berlin. _____
5. People eat meat at the Thai festival. _____
6. The garlic festival lasts for 21 days. _____

> ask**&** _____
> **ANSWER**
> Gilroy, California, is famous for its garlic. What is your city or country famous for?

4 Language Link

The simple present: *Yes/No* questions and short answers

 A Study the chart. Notice the questions and answers.

Yes/No questions			Positive answers	Negative answers
Do	you		Yes, I do.	No, I don't.
	they	like garlic?	Yes, they do.	No, they don't.
Does	he		Yes, he does.	No, he doesn't.
	she		Yes, she does.	No, she doesn't.

B Pair work. **Complete the questions and statements. Check your answers with a partner.**

1. __Do__ you like Japanese food? Yes, _____.

2. _____ you eat a lot of junk food? No, _____.

3. _____ they speak English? Yes, _____.

4. _____ England have a queen? Yes, _____.

5. _____ he have breakfast every day? No, _____.

6. _____ the teacher speak Spanish? Yes, _____.

7. _____ your partner cook well? No, _____.

8. _____ your family eat lunch together? No, _____.

C Pair work. **Complete the conversation. Use the verbs to make questions. Practice the conversation with a partner.**

A: Hello. I'm Doctor Wilson. What is the problem?

B: I feel very tired, doctor.

A: _____ Do you eat _____ (eat) breakfast every day?

B: No, _____.

A: I see. _____ (smoke)?

B: Yes, _____.

A: _____ (eat) a lot of junk food?

B: Yes, _____.

A: _____ (exercise)?

B: No, _____.

5 Writing
My favorite food

A Do you have a favorite food? What is it? Where is it from? Write 3 or 4 sentences about it on a separate piece of paper.

B Group work. Read your writing to a group of classmates.

My favorite dish is called paella. This dish is from Spain. People eat it for lunch and dinner. It has rice, chicken, fish, onions, tomatoes, and a spice called saffron. It's delicious!

6 Communication
Health habits and food customs

A Complete one side of the chart with your information. Check (✓) *Yes* or *No*.

	Me		My Partner	
Health Habits	Yes	No	Yes	No
I have breakfast every day.				
I exercise.				
I drink three to four glasses of water every day.				
I go to sleep late every night.				
I eat a lot of junk food.				
I drink a lot of soda.				
I don't smoke.				
I take vitamins.				
I _____.				
I _____.				

B Pair work. Ask your partner questions. Complete the chart with his or her information. Is your partner a healthy person or an unhealthy person?

Do you have breakfast every day?

Yes, I do! I have toast and coffee.

C Pair work. Change partners. Tell your new partner about the information in your chart.

 Check out the World Link video.   **Practice your English online at** http://elt.thomson.com/worldlink

1 Vocabulary Link

This is my family!

 Marina

A Match each word with a person in the pictures.

Marina's . . .
a. father
b. brother
c. grandfather

Jenny's . . .
d. husband
e. son
f. grandmother

Yong Min's . . .
g. wife
h. daughter

Taylor's . . .
i. mother
j. sister

Jenny

Yong Min

Taylor

> In my family, there are five people—my father, my mother, my sister . . .

B Pair work. Discuss the questions with a partner.

1. How many people are there in your family?
2. Do you know any famous families? Name the people in the families.

2 Listening

Who is the speaker?

 A Listen and look at the pictures on page 56. Number the speakers in the order that you hear. (CD 1, Track 39)

Marina	Yong Min	Jenny	Taylor

 B Listen again. Complete the sentences. (CD 1, Track 40)

1. Emily is Taylor's _____ .
2. Eun Ha is Yong Min's _____ .
3. Pablo is Marina's _____ .
4. Alex is Jenny's _____ .

3 Pronunciation

Linking with 's

 A Listen to and practice saying the possessive form of these names. (CD 1, Track 41)

Men's names: Josh's Jin-song's Akira's
Women's names: Beth's Maria's Trish's

B Now practice saying the names in A with these words.

aunt	uncle	sister	son

Josh's aunt, Beth's uncle, . . .

C Group work. Play the role of a person in B. Introduce yourself to people in your group.

Hi, my name is Yuko. I'm Josh's aunt.

Hi, Yuko. I'm Peter. I'm Beth's uncle. Nice to meet you!

World Link

When people say "Uncle Sam," they are talking about the U.S. government.

uh-huh = yes
dad = father   mom = mother
parents = mother and father
grandparents = grandmother and
grandfather

 A Listen to the conversation.
(CD 1, Track 42)

Marina:	Taylor, is this your family?
Taylor:	Uh-huh.
Marina:	Who's this?
Taylor:	This is my sister. And this is my mom.
Marina:	What's your sister's name?
Taylor:	Emily. Do you have any brothers or sisters?
Marina:	Yes. I have an older brother.

B Pair work. **Practice the conversation with a partner.**

C Group work. **Join another pair. Ask your group: Do you have any brothers or sisters? Complete the chart below.**

Useful Expressions:
Asking and answering about family
Do you have any brothers or sisters?
Yes. I have a sister.
Yes. I have an older brother.
Yes. I have two brothers and one sister.
No. I'm an only child.

Pablo   Luis

Anita's family photo

Classmate's name	Brothers/Sisters?	Names
Anita	2 brothers	Pablo, Luis

D Class activity. **Tell the class about one person in your group.**

Anita has two brothers. Their names are . . .

5 Language Link

Possessives

 A **Study the chart. Notice the use of ' and 's.**

singular noun + 's	Taylor is	**Emily's** brother.
	Taylor is	**her** brother.
	Louis's wife	is Carol.
	His wife	is Carol.
plural noun + '	**My parents'**	house is small.
	Their	house is small.
irregular plural noun + 's	**The children's**	names are Emily and John.
	Their	names are Emily and John.

B **Make the singular and plural nouns possessive. Add 's or '.**

1. (James) __James's__ cell phone

2. (Yong Min) _____ mother

3. (girls) the _____ CD player

4. (baby) the _____ father

5. (babies) the _____ food

6. (bus) the _____ radio

C **Look at Taylor's family tree. Complete the sentences.**

1. Taylor is __Emily's__ brother.

2. Susan is _____ sister.

3. Carol is _____ wife.

4. Todd is _____ husband.

5. Carol and Louis are _____ parents.

6. Susan has two sons. Her _____ names are Taylor and John.

7. Todd and Susan have three children. The _____ names are Taylor, Emily, and John.

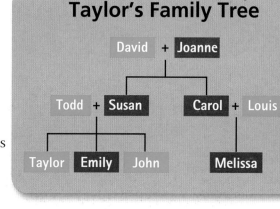

Taylor's Family Tree

David + Joanne

Todd + Susan   Carol + Louis

Taylor   Emily   John   Melissa

 D **Read the sentences. Cross out the underlined words and write his, her, or their.**

Her
Taylor: "~~My aunt's~~ name is Carol. My uncle's name is Louis. My cousin's name is Melissa."

Carol: "My niece's name is Emily. My nephews' names are Taylor and John."

aunt (female)
niece (female)
uncle (male)
nephew (male)
cousin (male or female)

6 Communication

My partner's family tree

 Pair work. Interview a partner. Complete the questionnaire.

What is/are . . .

1. your father's father's name? ___His name is_____
2. your father's mother's name? ___Her name is_____
3. your mother's father's name? _____
4. your mother's mother's name? _____
5. your parents' names? _____
6. your father's brothers' and sisters' names? _____
   ☐ He has no brothers or sisters.
7. your mother's brothers' and sisters' names? _____
   ☐ She has no brothers or sisters.
8. your brothers' and sisters' names? _____
   ☐ My partner has no brothers or sisters.
9. the names of other people in your family?

_____

B **Draw your partner's family tree.**

A Family Tree

C **Pair work. Show your partner the family tree you made. Ask your partner to check the information.**

Your older brother's name is Felix, right?

No, my older brother's name is Fernando!

My Family

1 Vocabulary Link

Family relationships

 A Use words from the box to complete the sentences. Use each word only once.

a. married *(adj)*
b. single *(adj)*
c. ~~divorced~~ *(adj)*
d. single parent *(n)*
e. stepfather *(n)*
f. stepdaughter *(n)*
g. large *(adj)*

Margo   Craig

1. Margo and Craig are ___divorced___.

Jane   Craig

2. Jane lives with her father, Craig. Craig is a _____.

Liam

3. Jane's parents are divorced.
   Liam is Jane's _____.
   Jane is Liam's _____.

The Nielsen Family

4. This is a _____ family.

Woojin   Nayen

5. Woojin and Nayen are _____.

Tomás

6. Tomás is _____.

 B Pair work. **Discuss the questions with a partner.**

1. Are you married or single?
2. What do you think of Jane's family? Are families like this common in your country?
3. Are families changing in your country? Explain your answer.

2 Listening

Three families

 A Listen. Are the women married or single? Check (✓) the correct boxes for items 1 and 2. (CD 1, Track 43)

	Sonia	Rachel	Monika
1. She is married.	☐	☐	☐
2. She is divorced.	☐	☐	☐
3. She is a housewife.	☐	☐	☐
4. She has two children.	☐	☐	☐
5. She has three children.	☐	☐	☐
6. She has a stepdaughter.	☐	☐	☐
7. Her children visit their dad on weekends.	☐	☐	☐
8. Her husband is from another country.	☐	☐	☐

 B Listen again. Check (✓) the correct boxes for items 3-8. (CD 1, Track 44)

3 Reading

How big is your family?

A Read the messages and circle the correct answers below.

 Hello, everyone! My name is Mayumi Tanaka. I am twenty-five years old. I live with my father, Hisashi, and mother, Akiko, in Tokyo. We're a very small family, and I am an only child. How big is your family?

 Greetings from the United States! My name is Paul Martin. In my family there are four children. My parents are divorced. My mom, Kimberly, is married to my stepfather, Francis. They have one son—my half-brother, Zack. My dad's name is Tom. His new wife is Elaine. They have two daughters—my half-sisters, Erica and Annie. They're twins. It's a big family!

Hello there! My name is Alex Martinez. I live with my wife, Lara, in Mexico City. We have two children. My daughter, Carmen, is twenty-seven. She is married to a great guy named Victor. They have one son, Marcos. We also have a son, Javier. He is a university student. He's single.

1. Who is a grandfather?	Paul	Mayumi	Alex
2. Who has no brothers and sisters?	Paul	Mayumi	Alex
3. Who has a stepmother and a stepfather?	Paul	Mayumi	Alex

B Read the messages again. Complete the family charts for Mayumi, Paul, and Alex.

Mayumi's family	Paul's family	Alex's family
Mayumi's mother: ____Akiko____	Paul's father: _____	Alex's _____: Lara
_____: Hisashi	_____: Elaine	Alex and Lara's _____: Javier
	Paul's half-sisters: _____	Alex and Lara's _____: Carmen
	_____: Kimberly	Carmen's _____: Victor
	Paul's stepfather: _____	_____: Marcos
	Paul's _____: Zack	
Number in Mayumi's family: ____	Number in Paul's family: ____	Number in Alex's family: ____

ask**&**
ANSWER
In your country, are most families large or small?
Do you know a very large family?

4 Language Link

Numbers 11–2,000

World Link

The average household in Saudi Arabia has more than 7 people.

Source: *The Economist Pocket World in Figures, 2003*

A Say the numbers with your teacher.

11 eleven	20 twenty	30 thirty	100 one hundred
12 twelve	21 twenty-one	40 forty	200 two hundred
13 thirteen	22 twenty-two	50 fifty	300 three hundred
14 fourteen	23 twenty-three	60 sixty	
15 fifteen	24 twenty-four	70 seventy	1,000 one thousand
16 sixteen	25 twenty-five	80 eighty	2,000 two thousand
17 seventeen	26 twenty-six	90 ninety	
18 eighteen	27 twenty-seven		
19 nineteen	28 twenty-eight		
	29 twenty-nine		

1918 = nineteen eighteen
2005 = two thousand five

B Say the years.

1492   1789   1848   1905   1956   1969   1977   1984   1990   2001   2004

C Pair work. When were these people born? Write the year.
Then ask and answer questions with a partner.

Linda: 72 years old   Born: _____   *How old is Linda?*

Mikhail: 45 years old   Born: _____

Cameron: 26 years old   Born: _____   *She's 72. She was born in 19____.*

Akemi: 1 year old   Born: _____

You ____ years old   Born: _____

Game: BINGO! Read the directions and play.

1. Write different numbers from the chart on page 63 on your bingo card.
2. The teacher says numbers.
3. Write an X on the numbers you hear.
4. When all numbers have an X, say BINGO!

5 Writing

About my family

 Write a letter to a pen pal from another country. Tell your pen pal about your family.

Dear Keiko,

My name is Paolo Gasbari. My family is small. I live with my parents in Milan, Italy. My father is fifty-five and my mother is fifty. My sister's name is Dorothea. She is twenty-seven. She is married. I am twenty, and I'm single.

B Pair work. Exchange letters with a partner. Are your families similar or different? Tell the class.

6 Communication

Famous people

 A Who are these famous people? When were they born? Unscramble the years and write their ages. Check your answers on page 154.

Born: _____ (4591) Age: ___

Born: <u>1930</u> (3910) Age: ___

Born: _____ (5981) Age: ___

Born: _____ (7951) Age: ___

Born: _____ (0619) Age: ___

Born: _____ (1289) Age: ___

ask& _____
ANSWER
Where is the person from?
How old is the person now?
Is this person single or married?

 B Group work. **Game: Who am I?**

1. Think of a famous person. Don't tell anyone! Answer the questions below.

   Is it a man or a woman? _____

   Where is the person from? _____

   How old is the person? _____

   Is the person single or married? _____

   Who are some people in the person's family? _____

2. Tell your group about your person. Do not say the person's name. Your group guesses the person.

   This is a man. He is from England. His father's name is Charles.

   I know! It's Prince William!

 Check out the World Link video.   **Practice your English online at** http://elt.thomson.com/worldlink

Lesson B • Families, big and small **65**

REVIEW: Units 4-6

A Pair work. Tony and Paloma are in a café.
Complete the conversation.

B Pair work. Practice the conversation with a partner.

C Pair work. Change roles and practice the conversation again.

2 See it and say it

A Pair work. **Study the picture below for 15 seconds. Then close your book. What are the people doing? Tell your partner.**

B Pair work. **Talk about the picture.**

- In the food court, there is food from different countries. Name the countries.
- Which place has a "lunch special"?
- What are the people eating and drinking?

C Pair work. **Choose a place to eat lunch. Explain your choice.**

> I like Gino's. They have pizza.

> That's OK with me—I love pizza!

D Pair work. **Two people are entering the food court. What are they saying? Role-play a short conversation.**

3 Odd word out

For number 1, *teacher* is different.

Pair work. **Look at the groups of words. Circle the one that's different in each group. Tell your partner.**

1. mother	father	(teacher)	daughter
2. tea	soda	milk	sandwich
3. math	singing	business	English literature
4. fast food	breakfast	lunch	dinner
5. knife	chopsticks	glass	fork
6. mother	sister	aunt	nephew
7. listening to music	studying for a test	dancing	playing tennis
8. cake	ice cream	fish	chocolate

4 He speaks Spanish.

A Pair work. **Look at the items in one person's backpack. What do you know about this person? Make sentences. Use the verbs in parentheses.**

1. (be) __His name is Brian Hughes__ .
2. (speak) __He speaks Spanish__ .
3. (be) _____ .
4. (go) _____ .
5. (like) _____ .
6. (play) _____ .
7. (have) _____ .
8. (study) _____ .

B Pair work. **Write four questions to ask your partner. Use the verbs in the box. Then, take turns asking and answering questions.**

> like   hate   study   listen to   live   have   go   speak   drive   play

Do you play an instrument?

Yes, I do. I play the guitar and the piano.

1. _____
2. _____
3. _____
4. _____

5 Listening: It's his birthday.

A Sophie and her friend are talking. Listen.
Choose the correct answers. (CD1, Track 45)

1. Sophie's _____ are visiting from Mexico.
   a. parents   b. grandparents   c. brothers

2. It's Sophie's _____ birthday.
   a. father's   b. grandfather's   c. brother's

3. How old is he?
   a. 50   b. 60   c. 70

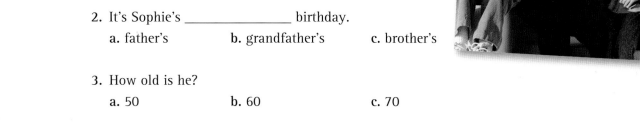

 B Listen again. Circle the correct family tree. (CD1, Track 46)

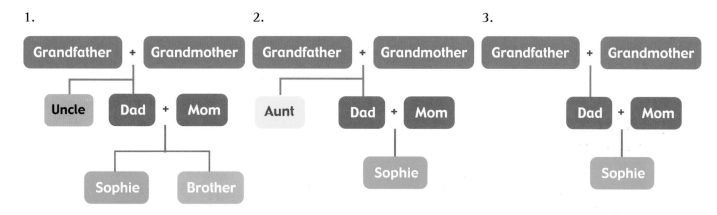

6 What's wrong?

A Are these questions true or false? Write T or F. Then correct the
underlined words and numbers to make the false sentences true.

```
+   plus
-   minus
=   equals
```

_____ 1. A person born on January 1, 1984, is <u>eighteen</u> years old.

_____ 2. Your brother's daughter is your <u>cousin</u>.

_____ 3. 37 + 22 = <u>sixty</u>.

_____ 4. Your father's sister is your <u>aunt</u>.

_____ 5. John is forty-five years old. He was born in <u>1956</u>.

_____ 6. Your sister's son is your <u>uncle</u>.

_____ 7. 100 – 24 = <u>seventy-three</u>.

_____ 8. Your aunt's son is your <u>nephew</u>.

_____ 9. Here is a pattern: three, six, nine, twelve, <u>fourteen</u>, eighteen, twenty-one, twenty-four.

_____ 10. Your parents are divorced. Your father marries again. His new wife is your <u>stepmother</u>.

 B Check your answers on page 154. You get 1 point for each correct
answer. How many points do you have?

Time

Lesson A | Time and schedules

1 Vocabulary Link

What time is it?

 A Look at the pictures of Alberto's day and listen to the times. (CD 2, Track 1)

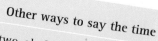

Other ways to say the time

2:05 = two-oh-five OR five past two
2:15 = two-fifteen OR a quarter past two
2:30 = two-thirty OR half past two
2:45 = two-forty-five OR a quarter to three

It's seven o'clock in the morning.

It's eight-fifteen.

It's eight forty-five.

It's noon.

It's two-thirty in the afternoon.

It's eight-oh-five in the evening.

It's ten-ten at night.

It's midnight.

 B Pair work. Take turns asking the time with a partner.

1.
2.
3.

4.
5.
6.

What time is it ?

It's five past four.

2 Listening

Oh no . . . we're late!

  A Listen. Number the pictures as you listen. (CD 2, Track 2)

It's a Dinner Party!

Please join us...

Name: _____
1. Ⓐ Ⓑ Ⓒ Ⓓ
2. Ⓐ Ⓑ Ⓒ Ⓓ
3. Ⓐ Ⓑ Ⓒ Ⓓ
4. Ⓐ Ⓑ Ⓒ Ⓓ
5. Ⓐ Ⓑ Ⓒ Ⓓ
6. Ⓐ Ⓑ Ⓒ Ⓓ
7. Ⓐ Ⓑ Ⓒ Ⓓ
8. Ⓐ Ⓑ Ⓒ Ⓓ
9. Ⓐ Ⓑ Ⓒ Ⓓ
10. Ⓐ Ⓑ Ⓒ Ⓓ

NO. 1 BOX OFFICE HIT!

THE TYRANT

NOW SHOWING
AT A THEATER NEAR YOU.

Time now	Starting time	Time now	Starting time	Time now	Starting time
☐ 6:15	☐ 7:00	☐ 1:15	☐ 1:00	☐ 7:15	☐ 7:30
☐ 6:50	☐ 10:00	☐ 12:45	☐ 12:00	☐ 7:50	☐ 8:30

  B Listen again. Check (✓) the correct times above. (CD 2, Track 3)

 C Pair work. Tell your partner about each picture.

> The movie starts at . . . Now, it's . . .

3 Pronunciation 🔤

Numbers

  A Listen and repeat the numbers. (CD 2, Track 4)

19   90   18   80   17   70   16   60   15   50   14   40   13   30

  B Listen to the sentences. Circle the correct answer. (CD 2, Track 5)

1. John's plane arrives at 1:14 / 1:40.
2. Pilar was born in 1918 / 1980.
3. Class ends at 2:15 / 2:50.
4. My walk to school takes 19 / 90 minutes.
5. Each concert ticket is 16 / 60 dollars.
6. Hiro drives 17 / 70 miles to work every day.
7. Martin's daughter is 13 / 30 years old.

  C Listen and check your answers. (CD 2, Track 6)

Let's see a movie.

A Listen to the conversation. Underline the names of the movies. (CD 2, Track 7)

Adriano:	Here's the newspaper, Jessie.
Jessie:	Great. What movies are playing?
Adriano:	The new Star Wars movie is playing at 2:00. Let's see it!
Jessie:	Hmm . . . I don't really want to see that.
Adriano:	Okay. Then let's see The Lord of the Rings III.
Jessie:	Okay, that sounds good!

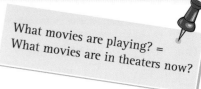

What movies are playing? = What movies are in theaters now?

B Pair work. Practice the conversation with a partner.

C Think of two movies. Write them on the lines.

_____

_____

D Pair work. Ask your partner to go to a movie with you.

Useful Expressions:
Suggestions with *Let's*
Let's see the new *Star Wars* movie. Hmm . . . I don't really want to see that.
Then let's see *The Lord of the Rings III.* Okay, that sounds good!

Let's see the new Batman *movie.*

Hmm... I don't really want to see that.

E Pair work. Switch roles and practice again.

World Link

India now produces more feature-length movies than any other country in the world — over 800 a year!

Source: *Guiness Book of World Records*

5 Language Link

Prepositions of time: *in/on/at;* question word *when*

When is your class?

It's on Monday.
on Monday morning.
at 8 o'clock.
in the morning.

 A Complete the sentences with *in, on,* or *at.*

1. My favorite show is on TV ____at____ 9:00.
2. Jessie's class is _____ the evening _____ 7:30.
3. I'm busy _____ the afternoon. Let's study _____ the morning _____ 10:00.
4. _____ Sunday, the market opens _____ 12:00 and closes _____ 6:00.

B Look at Adriano's schedule for this week. Write three different answers to the questions below.

Monday	Tuesday	Wednesday	Thursday	Friday	Saturday	Sunday
	12:00 study group		*12:00 study group*	*9:10 math test*		*My birthday!*
		2:45 doctor's appointment			*1:15 guitar lesson*	
	5:30 dance class		*5:30 dance class*		*8:00 Carla's party*	

1. When is Adriano's doctor's appointment?
   It's on Wednesday. It's at 2:45. It's in the afternoon.

2. When is Adriano's dance class?
   _____

3. When is Adriano's math test?
   _____

 C Pair work. Ask your partner one more question about Adriano's schedule. Then your partner asks you one more.

 ask**&**
ANSWER
What is your favorite day of the week? Why?
What day is today?
What day was yesterday?
What day is tomorrow?

6 Communication

What's on TV?

 A Look at these popular American TV shows. Do you know them?

Rugrats

The Planet's Funniest Animals

E.R.

Friends

Cops

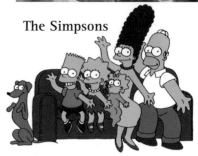
The Simpsons

B What is each show about? Match a show with a description.

Name of show	The show is about . . .
__d__ 1. *E.R.*	a. a cartoon family
_____ 2. *Friends*	b. police and crime
_____ 3. *Rugrats*	c. babies—a children's cartoon
_____ 4. *The Simpsons*	d. people working in a hospital
_____ 5. *The Planet's Funniest Animals*	e. six friends in New York City
_____ 6. *Cops*	f. animals doing funny things

C When are the six shows above on TV? Say the time and channel.

> *Friends is on TV at 8:00. It's on channel 4.*

The Paper TV TODAY

Thursday

Channel	7:00 PM	7:30	8:00	8:30	9:00	9:30	10:00
4	News		Friends	Scrubs	Will & Grace	Good Morning Miami	E.R.
5	News		Survivor		CSI – Crime Scene Investigation		The Sopranos
Animal Planet	Funniest Animals	Amazing Animal Videos	Animal Babies		The Crocodile Hunter		Animal Cops
NICK	Hey Arnold	Rugrats	The Wild Thornberrys		The Cosby Show		Star Trek
WPN	Seinfeld	The Simpsons	Joe Millionaire		Who Wants to be a Millionaire?		Cops

 D Pair work. Do you know these shows? Do you like them? Tell your partner.

Time

Lesson B | It's the weekend!

1 Vocabulary Link

Weekend activities

A Look at the weekend activities.
Match an activity with a picture.

a. relax
b. go shopping
c. work
d. go to the movies
e. go out with friends
f. work out at the gym
g. spend time with family
h. take a trip somewhere

B Pair work. Discuss the questions with a partner.

1. Do you like these activities?
2. What other activities do you like to do?

> I like to go to the movies and work out at the gym.

2 Listening

Do you have plans for the weekend?

 A Listen. Complete the sentence. (CD 2, Track 8)

Nick is probably Kelly's _____.
a. brother   b. classmate   c. husband

 B Listen again. Check (✓) the correct activities for each person. (CD 2, Track 9)

	spend time with family	go out with friends	go to the movies	work out at the gym	relax
Nick	☐	☐	☐	☐	☐
Kelly	☐	☐	☐	☐	☐

  C Listen again. Circle the correct choices. (CD 2, Track 10)

Nick asks Kelly to meet his friend / see a movie / visit his family tonight at 8:45 / 9:00 / 9:15.

3 Reading

What do you do on the weekend?

 What do you usually do on the weekends?

 A Read the article on page 77. Complete the sentences.

1. Marco doesn't go to school on ____C____ .
   a. Saturday
   b. Sunday
   c. both a and b

2. Hee Jin works on _____ .
   a. Saturday
   b. Sunday
   c. both a and b

3. In Ali's country, the weekend is on _____ .
   a. Thursday and Friday
   b. Friday and Saturday
   c. Saturday and Sunday

4. _____ studies on Sunday.
   a. Marco
   b. Hee Jin
   c. Ali

World Link

In most Islamic countries, the work week is Saturday through Wednesday.

B Read the newspaper column.

 World Link PRESS

The Question Lady wants to know...
What do you do on the weekend?

Marco: Lima, Peru

On the weekend, I don't do anything special – I relax. On Saturday morning, I sleep late. In the evening, I go out with my girlfriend. We go to the movies or go out for dinner. On Sunday, I spend time with my family. We have a big meal together in the afternoon.

Hee Jin: Melbourne, Australia

What do I do? Well, I work on Saturday from 9:00 to 1:00 in an office. After work, I go shopping for a couple of hours. Saturday night is usually "girls' night out" – I go out with my friends to the clubs. On Sunday, I work out at the gym or go to a movie.

Ali: Seattle, Washington, USA

I'm from Saudi Arabia, and in my county, the weekend is on Thursday and Friday. Back home, I spend time with my family. Now, I'm a university student in the United States. Things are different. On Saturday, I take a trip somewhere. Sometimes, I see different places in this city with friends or by myself. On Sunday, I study. I'm an engineering student, and I have a lot of homework!

 C What do the people do on the weekend?
Check (✓) the activities.

	sleeps late	works out	studies	goes out for dinner	sees a movie	takes a trip	spends time with family	goes shopping	works
Marco	☐	☐	☐	☐	☐	☐	☐	☐	☐
Hee Jin	☐	☐	☐	☐	☐	☐	☐	☐	☐
Ali	☐	☐	☐	☐	☐	☐	☐	☐	☐

 D Pair work. Tell your partner about Marco's, Hee Jin's, and Ali's weekend activities.

ask **&**
ANSWER

What are some interesting things to do on the weekend?

The simple present: *wh-* questions

 A Study the chart. Then match a question with the correct response.

Wh- word	*do/does*	subject	verb	Answers
Where	do	you	live?	(I live) in London, England.
	does	she		(She lives) in Sao Paulo, Brazil.
What	do	you	do on the weekend?	I go out with my friends.
	does	she		She spends time with her family.

1. What do you have for breakfast?
2. Who do you live with?
3. Where do you live?
4. When do you have class?
5. Who does Jane live with?
6. Where does Mary go to school?
7. What does John study?
8. When does Michael have class?

a. She lives with her sister.
b. He studies French.
c. I live with a roommate.
d. I have class on Monday.
e. I have cereal.
f. He has class at 10:00.
g. I live in Portland, Oregon.
h. She goes to Stanford University.

 B Read about Elaine's weekend. Answer the questions.

On Saturday, she . . .	On Sunday, she . . .
• works at a furniture store in the morning. • relaxes in the afternoon. • goes out with her boyfriend in the evening.	• goes shopping with her sister in the morning. • works out at the gym in the afternoon. • e-mails her friends in the evening.

1. What does Elaine do on Saturday afternoon? ___She relaxes.___
2. When does she work? _____
3. Where does she work? _____
4. What does Elaine do on Saturday evening? _____

C Pair work. Look at Elaine's Sunday schedule. Write four more questions. Ask your partner.

1. _____
2. _____
3. _____
4. _____

5 Writing

My weekend

 Read about Jean-Claude's weekend. Then write about your weekend. What do you do?

 Pair work. Share your writing with a partner.

My name is Jean-Claude. I'm a senior at an international high school in Nancy, France. In my country, the weekend is on Saturday and Sunday. On Saturday afternoon, I relax or play soccer with my classmates. On Saturday night, I go out with my friends. We go to the movies or a café. On Sunday, I study or spend time with my family. What do you do?

6 Communication

Find someone who . . .

A Read the questions on the left side of the chart. In the "Me" column, check (✓) the activities you do.

What do you do on the weekends?

Do you . . .	Me	Classmate	Question	Details
watch TV?			What . . . ?	
go shopping?			Where . . . ?	
go to bed late?			When . . . ?	
go out with friends?			Where . . . ?	
study?			What . . . ?	
work out at the gym?			Where . . . ?	
go to clubs?			Who . . . ?	

B Class activity. Interview your classmates. For each question, find a different person to answer *Yes*. Write the classmate's name. Ask another question to get more details.

Do you watch TV on the weekend?

Yes, I do.

What do you watch?

On Sunday night, I watch The Simpsons.

 Check out the World Link video. **Practice your English online at** http://elt.thomson.com/worldlink

1 Vocabulary Link

What's the date today?

A Put the months in order (1–12).
Then say them with your teacher.

Months of the year

_____ March   _____ September   _____ February

_____ December   _____ May   _____ July

_____ October   _____ August   _____ November

__1__ January   _____ June   _____ April

B Pair work. Take turns saying the dates with your partner.

January 2	February 1	April 3
5/15/04	7/7/02	11/29

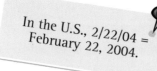

In the U.S., 2/22/04 = February 22, 2004.

Ordinal numbers

1st	first	16th	sixteenth
2nd	second	17th	seventeenth
3rd	third	18th	eighteenth
4th	fourth	19th	nineteenth
5th	fifth	20th	twentieth
6th	sixth	21st	twenty-first
7th	seventh	30th	thirtieth
8th	eighth	40th	fortieth
9th	ninth	50th	fiftieth
10th	tenth	60th	sixtieth
11th	eleventh	70th	seventieth
12th	twelfth	80th	eightieth
13th	thirteenth	90th	ninetieth
14th	fourteenth	100th	one hundredth
15th	fifteenth		

C Look at the American holidays below. Match each date with a holiday.

1. February 14   3. December 31
2. a Sunday in early spring   4. December 25

Christmas

Valentine's Day

Easter

New Year's Eve

D Pair work. What are important holidays in your country?
When are they? Discuss with your partner.

2 Listening

Independence Day

 A Listen to three people talk about Independence Day in their countries. Where is each speaker from? Check (✓) the correct country. (CD 2, Track 11)

1. ☐ The United States
   ☐ Great Britain

   Independence Day: _____

   Things that happen: _____

2. ☐ Spain
   ☐ Mexico

   Independence Day: _____

   Things that happen: _____

3. ☐ Russia
   ☐ Finland

   Independence Day: _____

   Things that happen: _____

  B Listen again. When is each country's Independence Day? Write the month and date. (CD 2, Track 12)

C Listen again. What things happen at Independence Day celebrations in these countries? Write the letter(s) in the chart. (CD 2, Track 13)

a. The president rings a bell.
b. People eat a special dinner.
c. People put candles in the window.

d. There is a fireworks show.
e. There are large parades.

3 Pronunciation

th and *t*

A Listen to the *th* and *t* sounds in these words. Then listen again and repeat. (CD 2, Track 14)

fourth / fort   eighth / ate   tenth / tent
math / mat   bath / bat   both / boat

B Listen and circle the word you hear. (CD 2, Track 15)

1. fourth   fort
2. math   mat
3. both   boat
4. eighth   ate
5. tenth   tent

 C Pair work. Say a word in A to your partner. Your partner points to it. Do this five times. Then switch roles.

A Pair work. Listen to the conversation. Then listen again and practice with a partner. (CD 2, Track 16)

Kendrick:	Hey Tanya, what's the date today?
Tanya:	It's November 3.
Kendrick:	When is Marty's birthday?
Tanya:	I don't know. I think it's on the fourth.
Kendrick:	Let's call and say "Happy Birthday!"
Tanya:	Okay. How old is he?
Kendrick:	I'm not sure. I think he's 21.

B Pair work. Make two new conversations and practice with your partner.
Use the new information below to change the red words in the conversation above.

1. Today's date: September 25
   Jasmine's birthday: September 27
   Her age: 18

2. Today's date: April 2
   Omar's birthday: April 1
   His age: 60

> **Useful Expressions:**
> **Saying you don't know**
>
> When is his birthday?
>   I don't know. I think it's on the fourth.
>
> How old is he?
>   I'm not sure. I think he's 21.

C Look at these famous people. How old are they? Match a person with a birthday. Then check your answers on page 154.

Birthdays
1. February 18, 1933   2. January 17, 1962   3. May 18, 1955   4. August 30, 1972

☐ Chow Yun Fat

☐ Cameron Diaz

☐ Jim Carrey

☐ Yoko Ono

ask & ANSWER
When is your birthday?
When is your mother's birthday?
When is your best friend's birthday?

How old is Chow Yun Fat?

I'm not sure. I think he's . . .

5 Language Link

Prepositions of time: *in* and *on*

The seasons
spring
summer
autumn/fall
winter

A Write the name of the season below each picture.

1. _____

2. _____

3. _____

4. _____

B Look at the question and the four answers.
Write four answers about yourself.

When were you born?   I was born **in January.**   1. _____

in 1984.   2. _____

in the winter.   3. _____

on January 1.   4. _____

C Complete the sentences with *in* or *on*.

1. My mother's birthday is _____ the winter. My father's birthday is _____ the fall.

2. Martin Luther King's birthday is _____ January. He was born _____ 1929.

3. The first day of spring is _____ March.

4. _____ the summer, Taylor visits his aunt and uncle in New York.

5. Schools are closed _____ Thanksgiving Day in the U.S.

6. When is Pablo's birthday? I think it's _____ the nineteenth of August.

ask**&**
ANSWER
What is your favorite season? Why?

on Christmas Day
on the twenty-fifth
of December

6 Communication

Special days

 A Write about your favorite day of the year.
Complete the chart about yourself.

	Me	My Partner
1. What is the special day?		
2. When is it?		
3. What do you eat or drink on that day?		
4. What do you do or where do you go?		

B Pair work. Interview a partner. Complete the chart with your partner's answers.

What is your favorite day?

*January 21st is my favorite day.
It's my birthday!*

C On some holidays or important days, there are expressions people say.

1. Look at the examples.

In the United States, people say . . .

I Love You!

on Valentine's Day

Happy Birthday!

on birthdays

Congratulations!

on graduation

Happy Mother's Day!

on Mother's Day

Merry Christmas!

on Christmas Day

Best Wishes!

on wedding days

2. Look again at the days in your chart in A. What do you say on these days?

 D Pair work. Take turns. Cover the page. Ask your partner
to say the expressions for the holidays above and others.

What do you say on Valentine's Day?

I love you!

Special Occasions

Lesson B | Holiday traditions

1 Vocabulary Link

Holiday photos

A Say the words below with your teacher.
Then complete the sentences with a word.
Use the **correct form.** (CD 2, Track 17)

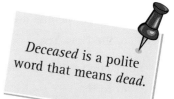

Deceased is a polite word that means *dead*.

---

relative (*n.*)   deceased (*adj.*)   remember (*v.*)   decorate (*v.*)   costume (*n.*)

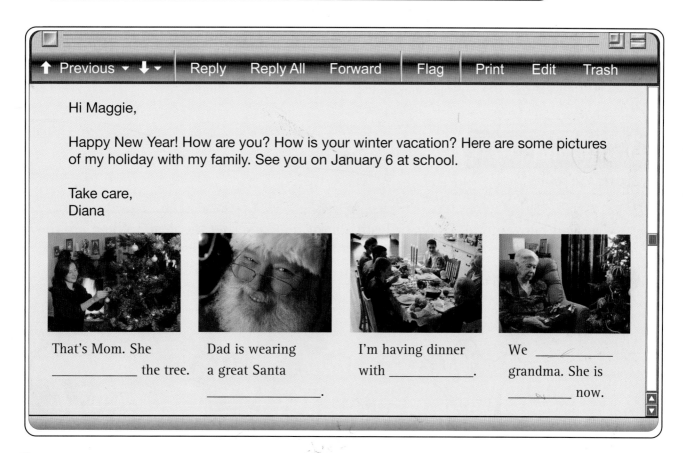

Previous ▼ ↓ ▼ | Reply Reply All Forward | Flag | Print Edit Trash

Hi Maggie,

Happy New Year! How are you? How is your winter vacation? Here are some pictures of my holiday with my family. See you on January 6 at school.

Take care,
Diana

That's Mom. She _____ the tree.

Dad is wearing a great Santa _____.

I'm having dinner with _____.

We _____ grandma. She is _____ now.

B Pair work. What do people do on New Year's Eve? On New Year's Day?
On Valentine's Day? Use the words below to talk about these and other holidays.

give gifts   make wishes   wear special clothes
spend time with family or friends   go to a parade   clean the house
decorate their homes   cook special foods   other _____

2 Listening

Two holidays

Happy New Year!

A Listen to the beginning of a conversation.
Answer the questions. (CD 2, Track 18)

1. What are Thanh and Janet talking about?
   a. the first day of spring
   b. things people do on December 31 and January 1
   c. the New Year

2. What country is Janet visiting?
   a. Korea
   b. Vietnam
   c. Japan

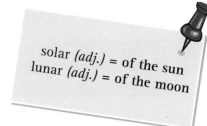

solar *(adj.)* = of the sun
lunar *(adj.)* = of the moon

B Now listen to the complete conversation.
Circle the correct answer. (CD 2, Track 19)

1. The Lunar New Year is on January 1 / every year on February 1 / in late January or early February.
2. People decorate their houses with a special food / gift / flower. It is a memory / symbol / day of spring.
3. On New Year's Eve, people make noise / are very quiet at midnight.

3 Reading

Ghosts and spirits

> Do you know any holidays or festivals for remembering the dead? When are they?

A Match a word with a picture.

a. witch   b. pumpkin   c. ghost   d. skeleton   e. skull   f. coffin

GHOSTS AND SPIRITS

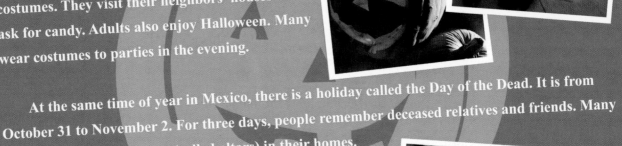

There are many interesting holidays in the United States. One of them is Halloween, the day the ghosts visit us. It's on October 31. But, Halloween is more about fun than fear. All over the U.S., people decorate their homes with pumpkins, black cats, and witches (the symbols of Halloween). On October 31, in the evening, children wear costumes. They visit their neighbors' houses and ask for candy. Adults also enjoy Halloween. Many wear costumes to parties in the evening.

At the same time of year in Mexico, there is a holiday called the Day of the Dead. It is from October 31 to November 2. For three days, people remember deceased relatives and friends. Many people make special tables (called altars) in their homes. They decorate the altars with candles, flowers, and photos. They give food and drink to the dead, and play their favorite music. People eat a special bread and candy skulls. In some places, there are also festivals. People wear skeleton costumes and carry a coffin through the town.

C Read each sentence below.
Write D (for Day of the Dead) or H (for Halloween). Write DH for both.

1. It's on October 31. _____
2. People wear costumes. _____
3. People eat candy skulls. _____
4. It's for three days. _____
5. There are festivals. _____
6. Children ask for candy. _____
7. People remember the dead. _____
8. People decorate their homes with pumpkins. _____

ask&
ANSWER
Do people wear costumes for other festivals or on other holidays?
When is the holiday or festival? What do people do?

How long; prepositions of time

A Study the chart. Then answer each question below in two ways.

When is the meeting?	It's at 7:00. It's from 7:00 to 9:00.
How long is the meeting?	It's from 7:00 to 9:00. It lasts for two hours.
How long does the meeting last?	It lasts for two hours. It's two hours long.

When do you study?	I study at night. I study from 5:00 to 8:00.
How long do you study?	I study from 5:00 to 8:00. I study for three hours.

1. How long is spring? (March 21–June 20)
   It's from March 21 to June 20 . It's three months long .

2. How long is the movie? (three hours)
   _____. _____.

3. How long is the Day of the Dead holiday? (three days)
   _____. _____.

4. How long does your winter break last? (December 15–January 6)
   _____. _____.

B Read the answers. Then write a question for each answer.

1. _____? My summer vacation lasts for three months—from June to August.
2. _____? The Vietnamese New Year lasts for seven days.
3. _____ every day? I exercise for two hours every day.
4. _____? The store is open from 10:00 a.m. to midnight.

An interesting holiday

A Read about the following Iranian holiday. Then write about an interesting holiday.
What is it called?
What is it for? When is it?
How long is it?
What do people do?

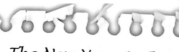

The New Year in Iran

In Iran, the New Year begins in March on the first day of spring. For the New Year, people make a special table. They put seven items on the table. Each item is a special symbol and starts with the "S" sound in the Persian language. Most people celebrate the New Year for thirteen days. They visit relatives and friends. They give gifts and eat special meals. On the thirteenth day of the New Year, people go out. It is bad luck to stay inside on this day.

B Pair work. Share your writing with a partner. Ask a question about your partner's holiday.

6 Communication

Holiday tickets

 A Pair work. **Look at the three holiday tickets. Together, choose an event to go to.**

Let's go to the . . .

$45.00
SEAT 4A

DOOR 1
ENTRANCE

NEW YEAR'S EVE CONCERT
The THREE TENORS
Luciano Pavarotti, Placido Domingo, Jose Carreras
THE SYDNEY OPERA HOUSE
FRIDAY, DECEMBER 31
9:00 - MIDNIGHT
SEAT 4A $45.00

Valentine's Day Double Feature!
The Alexandria Theater
Tuesday, February 14
Movie 1: *Titanic* with Leonardo DiCaprio
& Kate Winslet
6:00pm – 9:00pm
Movie 2: *Chocolat* with Juliette Binoche
& Johnny Depp
9:00pm – 11:00pm
$10.00

B Pair work. **Make a holiday ticket with a partner. Write your information below.**

EVENT:

WHEN (DATE AND TIME):

WHERE:

Kinds of events
a concert
a movie
a dance
a sports event
(tennis match,
basketball game)

Our ticket is for a Valentine's Day dance. It's on February 14. It's at 8:00 at the Blue Club.

C Group work. **Tell two pairs about your ticket. Ask about their tickets. Complete the chart.**

Event	Date and Time?	Where?
1.		
2.		

 Check out the World Link video. **Practice your English online at** http://elt.thomson.com/worldlink

1 Vocabulary Link

My daily schedule

 A Put the activities in order from 1–8 to describe your daily schedule.

get up   get dressed   check e-mail   go to bed   take a shower   do homework   work / go to school   get home

B Pair work. Tell your partner about your day. What things do you do? When do you do them?

> First, I get up at 7:00. Then I have breakfast and . . .

 C Read the information. Complete the sentences with the words in A.

Hi. I'm Stuart Powell. I'm an architect. I'm 29 and I'm married.

My day starts early. I _____ at 6:00 a.m. Then I _____ a shower and get _____.

At work, the first thing I do is _____. I usually have 40–50 e-mails in the morning! I _____ from 7:00 a.m. to 7:00 p.m. I _____ home at 7:30, and watch TV or read. I _____ at 11:00.

My name is Colleen Winton-Powell. I'm a nurse. My husband's name is Stuart. My day starts late. I _____ at 9:30 a.m. I _____ a shower and _____ dressed. I _____ from 3:00 p.m. to 11:00 p.m. at the hospital. I _____ home at midnight. My husband is usually sleeping. I watch TV and then I _____ at 1:00 or 1:30 a.m.

2 Listening

What's wrong?

 A Stuart and Colleen are talking. Listen.
Complete the sentence. (CD 2, Track 20)

Stuart and Colleen are _____.

a. making vacation plans

b. talking about their weekend schedules

c. spending time with their friends

 B Listen again.
Check (✓) the things Colleen and Stuart do on the weekend. (CD 2, Track 21)

	works all day	gets up late	goes shopping	goes to the gym	hangs out with friends
Colleen	☐	☐	☐	☐	☐
Stuart	☐	☐	☐	☐	☐

ASK & ANSWER

Do Stuart and Colleen see each other a lot? Explain your answer.
Stuart and Colleen are very busy people. Do you know any busy people?

3 Pronunciation

Sentence stress

 A Listen to the conversation. Notice the words that are stressed the most. (CD 2, Track 22)

A: Do you **usually** eat breakfast?

B: Yes, I **always** eat **breakfast**.

A: What do you **have**?

B: I **usually** have **eggs**.

 B Listen to the conversation. Underline the words with the most stress. (CD 2, Track 23)

A: Does he usually study at home?

B: No, he never studies at home.

A: Where does he study?

B: He always studies at the library.

 C Pair work. Practice the conversations in A and B with a partner. Pay attention to stress.

World Link

43% of Americans say they have no time to relax on the weekend.

Source: *The Shell Poll*™

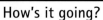

4 Speaking

How's it going?

  A Pair work. **Listen to the conversation.
Then practice with a partner.** (CD 2, Track 24)

Shannon:	Hey, Stuart. How's it going?
Stuart:	Okay, I guess.
Shannon:	What's wrong?
Stuart:	I'm unhappy. Colleen and I never spend time together.
Shannon:	Well, she works at night.
Stuart:	Yes, but on the weekend, she always hangs out with her friends. And she never helps with the housework.
Shannon:	Really?
Stuart:	Yeah. I always do the laundry. It's not fair.

 B Pair work. **Make three new conversations and practice with a partner.
Use the words below for the red words in the conversation above.**

1. So-so.
   I'm bored.
   goes shopping with her friends
   do the dishes

2. Don't ask!
   I'm angry.
   works out at the gym
   go grocery shopping

3. Not so great.
   I'm worried.
   goes on trips
   cook dinner

 C Class activity. **How are you today? Ask four people in your class.**

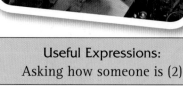

**Useful Expressions:
Asking how someone is (2)**

How's it going?	Great!
	Good.
	Not bad.
	Okay, I guess.
	So-so.
	Not so great.
	Don't ask!

 ask**&**
ANSWER

Who does the cleaning and shopping in your house?
Should both men and women do housework? Why or why not?

5 Language Link

Frequency adverbs

 A Study the chart. The frequency adverbs are in bold.
Underline the verbs in the chart.

With the verb *be*	Jackie is **always** late for class. *100%*
	usually
	often
	sometimes
	hardly ever
	never *0%*
With other verbs	Jackie **always** gets up at 8:00.

B Add the frequency adverb to each sentence.

always
1. He gets up at 7:30. (always)
    ^

2. Maria has cereal for breakfast. (never)

3. Javier is a happy person. (usually)

4. I hang out with friends on the weekend. (sometimes)

5. Dylan checks his e-mail in the morning. (often)

6. Colin is late for work. (hardly ever)

C Complete the sentences. Use the frequency adverb and the correct form of the verb.

1. Taylor (take a shower / never) _____never takes a shower_____ in the morning.
   He (take a shower / always) _____ at night.

2. Marie (go home / hardly ever) _____ for lunch.

3. The boutiques (be / always) _____ open on Sunday.

4. I (have dinner / often) _____ with my family.
   I (eat / sometimes) _____ with my friends.

5. Let's take a taxi to school. The bus (be / always) _____ late.

6. Michael (do homework / never) _____ at school. He does it at home.

 D Pair work. Ask and answer questions with a partner.
Use frequency adverbs in your answers.

When do you get up in the morning? Hang out with your friends?
What do you have for breakfast? Watch on TV at night?
Do you speak English outside of class? Eat lunch at home?

Let's talk

 A Pair work. Role play. Imagine you are a university student. You are looking for a roommate. Interview a classmate. Use the Roommate Questions.

Roommate Questions

1. When do you usually get up?
2. Do you sometimes get up late?
3. When do you usually check e-mail?
4. When do you usually go to bed?
5. Do you sometimes go to bed very late?
6. Where and when do you usually do homework?
7. What time do you usually go to work/school?
8. What time do you usually get home?
9. How often do you hang out with friends at home?
10. How often do you clean the house?
11. What time do you take a shower?
12. I always have breakfast at home. Do you?

> When do you usually get up?

> I usually get up at 7:00.

 B Pair work. Role play. Interview two more classmates.

 C Think about the three interviews. Who is the best roommate for you? Choose the best roommate, and tell the class his or her name. Explain your choice.

> Maria is the best roommate for me. We both get up early.

Person to Person

1 Vocabulary Link

Dating customs

A Read about dating customs around the world. Pay attention to the words in blue.

In North America, dating in high school is common. Many people go on a first date at the age of 16. At restaurants, they sometimes split the bill—each person pays 50%.

In Europe, dating customs are similar to the U.S. Many people begin to date in high school. They often go out together in groups. It is easy for people to meet each other this way.

In the Middle East, things are different. Parents often find a match for their son or daughter.

B Complete the sentences with the blue words from A.

1. Claudia and William are going to the movies together today.
   It's their third _____date_____.

2. In the U.S., John is a _____ first name.
   Many men have this name.

3. James and Trudi love movies, and they both like to exercise.
   They are a good _____.

4. The cost of the food is $20. Let's _____. Here is $10.

5. Ann wants to _____ a handsome, intelligent, rich man.

6. Todd is a night person. Celine is a day person. They are _____.

7. Simone and Dylan are very _____.
   They both study business, and they both like soccer.

8. Alan and Cindy often eat in restaurants together. Alan always _____.

ask & _____
ANSWER
When do people start to date in your country? What things do they do?

A Listen. Circle the correct words to complete each sentence. (CD 2, Track 25)

1. Connie and Tim are talking about marriage / dating / divorce.
2. Connie is single / dating someone / married.

  B Listen again. Circle the correct answer. (CD 2, Track 26)

1. Tim thinks Connie is / isn't dating Greg.
2. Connie dates / doesn't date Greg.
3. Connie thinks / doesn't think the Internet is a good place to find a boyfriend.
4. Tim uses / doesn't use a dating website.

World Link

In the U.S., when teens go on dates they often "go Dutch." This means that each person pays his or her own expenses.

ask&
ANSWER
Is the Internet a good way to meet people? Why or why not?

3 Reading

Who pays for dinner?

On a date, who usually pays for the meal or a movie? Why?

 A Read four people's opinions about dating on the next page.

 B Read the sentences. Who says each one?
Write Elena, In Ho, Erin, or Jason. Sometimes, more than one name is possible.

1. I always split the bill on a first date. _____
2. In my country, a man usually pays for the date. _____
3. In my country, friends go out in groups. You can meet someone that way. _____
4. On a date, I always pay. _____
5. My friend usually pays for her boyfriend. _____
6. When friends go out, each person pays for himself or herself. _____

ask&
ANSWER
Are your opinions similar to Elena's, In Ho's, Erin's, or Jason's? Explain. Describe a "perfect" date.

Dating: Who pays?

We are talking about dating with college students from the University of Washington. The question today: You are on a date at a nice restaurant.

Who pays for dinner?

Elena, Bogota, Colombia
"In my country, a man usually pays on a date. Here in the U.S., I think things are different. For example, my friend Beth is American. She and her boyfriend go out on the weekend. She often pays for movies and dinner for her boyfriend. She has a job and he doesn't. Maybe that's the reason."

In Ho, Pusan, Korea
"On a date in Korea, a man often pays, but sometimes the couple splits the bill. In Korea, it is also common for friends to go out together in a group. You can meet someone that way. In this case, each person pays for himself or herself."

Erin, Ottawa, Ontario, Canada
"Well, on a first date, I always split the bill with the other person. After that, sometimes he pays, and sometimes I pay. Elena's right."

Jason, Madison, Wisconsin, USA
"Like Erin said, it's common today to split the bill. But on a date, I always pay. I'm a traditional guy."

A Study the chart. Match a question with an answer or answers.

| Who | do | you | work | for? | ------- | (I work for) Toyota. |
| Who | ---- | ---- | works | for | Toyota? | I do. / She does. / Mr. Wada does. |

1. Who lives in Mexico?   _____c, e_____   a. He knows Mary.
2. Where do you live?   _____   b. I live in Paris.
3. What costs $1.50?   _____   c. I do.
4. What does the coffee cost?   _____   d. $1.50.
5. Who knows Stephan?   _____   e. Marco does.
6. Who does Stephan know?   _____   f. The coffee does.

B Three men want to date Mona. Read about them. Then answer the questions.

Mona
- goes to Boston University
- studies computer science
- likes dancing

Marc
- goes to Boston University
- studies business
- likes going to the movies

Steve
- goes to Boston University
- studies English
- likes dancing

Diego
- goes to New York University
- studies computer science
- likes going to a karaoke club

1. Who goes to New York University?   _Diego does_____.
2. What does Marc study?   _____.
3. Who goes to Boston University?   _____.
4. Who studies computer science?   _____.
5. Who studies English?   _____.
6. Who likes going to a karaoke club?   _____.
7. What does Marc like doing?   _____.
8. Who likes dancing?   _____.

ask& ANSWER

In your opinion, who is a good match for Mona? Why?

5 Writing

Modern dating

A Read the paragraph. Then write about modern dating customs.

In Switzerland, many young people date in high school. Teenagers often go out together in groups. It is easy to meet people this way. I am a university student now. On the weekend, I often go out with my friends. We go to a café or a club and meet people in these places. Sometimes I meet a girl I like. Then, I ask her out. On a date, we usually go to the movies or go dancing.

B Pair work. Share your writing with a partner. Ask two questions about your partner's writing.

6 Communication

Are we a good match?

A Complete the form with your information.

B Class activity. Interview three people. Use the form in A. Take notes.

find a friend!

Name

Age

A. Where do you usually meet people?

☐ at school   ☐ at a club

☐ at a party   ☐ at a restaurant or café

☐ on the Internet   other

B. Complete these sentences:

1. On the weekend, I always
2. On the weekend, I never
3. My favorite movie is
4. My favorite food is
5. In my free time, I

C Look at your notes. Is anyone similar to you? Write names in the chart.

Questions	Names
Who has the same interests as you?	
Who likes the same food as you?	
Who likes the same movies as you?	
Who does similar things on the weekend?	

Who has the same interests as you?

Javier does. We both listen to jazz.

 Check out the World Link video.   **Practice your English online at** http://elt.thomson.com/worldlink

Lesson B • Modern dating   **99**

1 Storyboard

A Group work. Get into a group of three. Alexis and Peter are at a movie theater. Complete the conversation.

B Group work. Practice the conversation.

C Group work. Change roles and practice the conversation again.

2 See it and say it

A Pair work. **Talk about the picture with a partner.**

- The people are at a party. Why?
- What's the date?
- What time is it?
- What's happening in the bedroom?
- What are the people doing in the living room?
- What are the people doing outside the house?
- On this holiday, what do you usually do?

B Pair work. **Choose one pair of people. Role-play a short conversation between the people.**

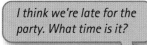

I think we're late for the party. What time is it?

It's . . .

3 Listening: Phone messages

A Imagine you have four messages on your answering machine. Listen to the messages. Then listen again. Write the day and time of each call. (CD 2 Track 27)

Message 1 - From: Jack

Day/Time: _____

Message: Let's _____
tonight.

Message 2 - From: Angela

Day/Time: _____

Message: Let's have _____
tomorrow at _____.

Message 3 - From: Doctor Miller's office

Day/Time: _____

Message: You have an appointment at
_____ on _____.

Message 4 - From: Richard

Day/Time: _____

Message: Let's _____ together on
_____ night.

B Listen again. Complete each phone message above. (CD 2 Track 28)

C Look at the phone messages. There is a problem with your schedule. What is it?

4 Culture Quiz: When and where?

A Pair work. Choose the correct answer with your partner. Use *I'm not sure,* *I think,* or *I don't know* as necessary.

1. In Japan, the school year starts in _____.
   a. January   b. April   c. September

2. In _____, people celebrate Christmas in the summer.
   a. Germany   b. Brazil   c. Hawaii

3. When is France's Independence Day?
   a. June 4   b. July 14   c. August 24

4. In Saudi Arabia, many people don't work on _____.
   a. Friday   b. Saturday   c. Sunday

5. In _____, there is sun at midnight in the summer.
   a. Mexico   b. Finland   c. England

6. In Iran, the New Year begins on _____.
   a. January 1   b. the first day of spring   c. the second of February

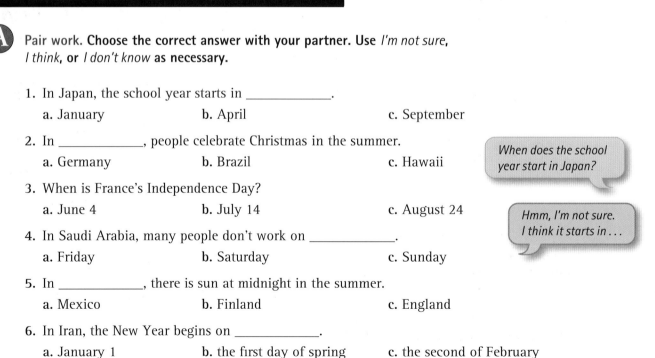

> When does the school year start in Japan?

> Hmm, I'm not sure. I think it starts in . . .

B Check your answers on page 154. For each correct answer, you get 5 points.

C Pair work. Compare your answers with another pair. Who has the most points?

5 Weekend activities

A Complete each sentence with your information.

On the weekend, I . . .

always	usually	often	sometimes	hardly ever	never	
☐	☐	☐	☐	☐	☐	get up early.
☐	☐	☐	☐	☐	☐	hang out with friends.
☐	☐	☐	☐	☐	☐	see a movie.
☐	☐	☐	☐	☐	☐	do my laundry.
☐	☐	☐	☐	☐	☐	go on a date.
☐	☐	☐	☐	☐	☐	practice my English.
☐	☐	☐	☐	☐	☐	spend time with my family.

B Pair work. Compare your answers with a partner's. Ask and answer questions. Are you similar or different?

A: I sometimes get up early on the weekend.
B: Really? I never get up early.
A: What time do you get up?
B: Usually around 10:00 or 11:00.
A: Wow! That's late!

6 Let's have a party!

A Plan a party. Make a party invitation on a separate piece of paper.

B Put your invitation on the classroom wall. Read the other invitations. Which parties are interesting to you? Choose three. Write the information for each one.

C Pair work. Compare your choices with a partner's. Together, choose one party.

D Class activity. Tell the class your choice. Why did you choose it?

Types of parties
dinner party
holiday party
birthday party
class party
costume party

You are invited to:

Date:
Time:
Place:

Phone:

Guest List:
- Mary Jo & Bob
- Kathy
- Yu Kim
- Yang & Jenny
- Maria & Carlos
- Kenichi
- Françoise & Marithe

We are going to Jane's birthday party on Friday night! There's live music, and . . .

1 Vocabulary Link

For rent

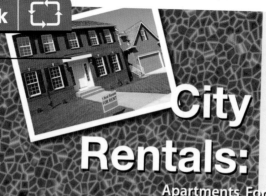

City Rentals:
Apartments For Rent

For rent:
1 bedroom
apartment
on the second
floor. $850
per month.

A Say the words in the box with your teacher. Then match each word with a place in the apartment.

a. living room

b. dining room

c. kitchen

d. bathroom

e. bedroom

f. balcony

g. yard

h. garage

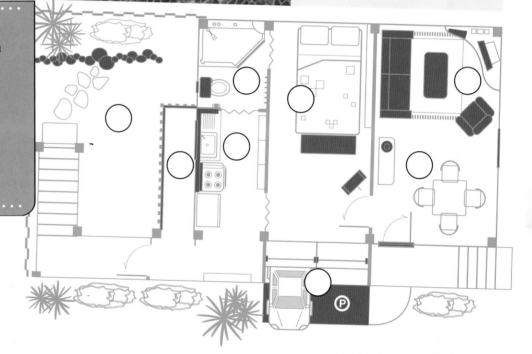

B Pair work. Complete the sentences about yourself. Tell a partner.

I live in an apartment. I live on the third floor. In my apartment, there are six rooms—a living room, a...

1. I live in an apartment / a house.

2. a. In my apartment building, I live on the _____ floor.

   b. In my house, my bedroom is on the _____ floor.

3. In my apartment or house, there are _____ rooms. (Name the rooms.)

ask&
ANSWER

What is your favorite room? Why is it your favorite?
In which room do you eat snacks? watch TV? relax? visit with people?

Apartment hunting

> In the first apartment, there is a kitchen . . .

 A Look at the pictures in B. What are the rooms in each apartment?

  B The man talks about three apartments. Number the apartments 1 to 3 as you listen. (CD 2, Track 29)

  C Listen again. What apartment does Ashley like?
Circle it. (CD 2, Track 30)

ANSWER

Imagine you are talking to the man at City Rentals. What apartment do you like? Why?
Do your friends live with their families or in their own apartments?

3 Pronunciation

Rising intonation to show surprise

  A Pair work. Listen to the conversations. Pay attention to the rising [↗] and falling [↘] intonation.
Then practice the conversations with a partner. (CD 2, Track 31)

A: How many rooms are there in your apartment?   A: Is there a garage?
B: Ten. [↘]   B: No. [↘]
A: Ten? [↗]   A: No? [↗]
B: Yeah.   B: No, but there's a yard.
A: Wow, you have a large apartment!

 B Pair work. Read the short conversations. Draw [↗] or [↘] in the correct place.
Then practice the conversations with a partner.

1. A: There are ten rooms in my apartment. [   ]   3. A: I live on a houseboat. [   ]
   B: Ten? [   ]   B. A houseboat? [   ]

2. A: It's too small. [   ]   4. A: It has twelve rooms. [   ]
   B: Too small? [   ]   B: Twelve rooms? [   ]

A Pair work. Listen to the conversation. Then practice with a partner. (CD 2, Track 32)

Justin:	Hi, Ashley.
Ashley:	Hi, Justin. Come in!
Justin:	Thanks. Hey, this is a nice apartment!
Ashley:	Yeah, and it's only $400 a month.
Justin:	Really? That's not bad! How many rooms are there?
Ashley:	There are five. There's a living room, a dining room, a kitchen, a bathroom, and my bedroom.
Justin:	Is there a garage?
Ashley:	No, but there's a small yard.
Justin:	That's great!

B Pair work. Make two new conversations and practice with your partner.
Use the words below for the red words in the conversation above.

1. Oh?
   Four rooms: a bedroom, a kitchen, a bathroom, and a living room

2. Wow!
   Six rooms: two bedrooms, a kitchen, a bathroom, a living room, and a dining room

Useful Expressions: Showing surprise
My house has ten bedrooms.
Really? That's big!
Wow!
Oh?

C Pair work.
1. Imagine you live in this place. Complete the information.

Number of rooms: _____
Kinds of rooms: _____
_____
_____
_____
_____

2. Create a conversation about the picture with a partner.
Use the conversation in A and the Useful Expressions to help you.

5 Language Link

There is/There are; How many

A Look at Ashley's apartment. Match the words with the items in the picture.

Furniture	Appliances
a. table	h. stove
b. chair	i. refrigerator
c. lamp	j. microwave
d. sofa	
e. mirror	
f. dresser	
g. bed	

> There's a table in the living room.
> There are chairs in the dining room.

B Pair work. Use *there is / there are* to talk about Ashley's apartment.

Student A: Tell your partner about the things in the living room and the dining room.

Student B: Tell your partner about the things in the bedroom and the kitchen.

C Pair work. Study the chart. Then complete the conversation with a partner.

Is there a table in the dining room?	Yes, **there is**. No, there isn't.
Are there (any) chairs in the dining room?	Yes, **there are**. No, there aren't (any).
How many chairs **are there** in the dining room?	(There's) one. (There are) four. There aren't any.

A: _____ rooms are there in your apartment, Ashley?

B: _____ five rooms.

A: _____ bedrooms are there?

B: _____ one.

A: _____ a garage?

B: No, _____, but _____ a small yard.

A: Really? How nice! _____ trees in the yard?

B: No, _____, but _____ flowers.

D Pair work. Talk about your apartment or house. Use the conversation in C to help you.

WorldLink

According to the Chinese practice of *feng shui*, the front door of a building should face east, in the direction of the rising sun.

Source: *Multicultural Manners: New Rules of Etiquette for a Changing Society.*

6 Communication

My favorite room

(A) Read about Ashley's bedroom. Pay attention to the words in bold.

Prepositions of place
in on under between behind
in front of next to in the middle of

In the middle of the room, there is a large rug. Next to the wall (on the right), there is a bed. There is a tennis racket between the bed and the wall. There is a soccer ball in front of the bed. There is a computer on the desk. Ashley's glasses are next to the computer. Next to her glasses (on the left) is a vase. There are flowers in the vase. Her dog is sleeping under the desk.

on the right
on the left

(B) Pair work. Look again at Ashley's room. She is looking for her backpack, CD player, and cell phone. Where is each thing in her room? Tell your partner.

(C) On a separate piece of paper, draw a floor plan of your favorite room. Draw the things in the room.

(D) Pair work. Show your floor plan to your partner. Tell him or her about it.

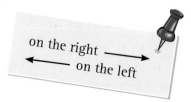

This is my bedroom. The door is here. There's a desk next to the wall, on the left. My bed is next to the desk. On my desk, there are...

108   Unit 10 • Home Sweet Home

Home Sweet Home

Lesson B | Student housing

1 Vocabulary Link

Housing choices

 A Imagine you want to study English at a school in Canada.
Read the advertisement. Pay attention to the words in red.

B Complete the sentences with the words in red in A.

1. Paloma is a student at the University of Michigan. She lives in a _____ on campus.
2. Please follow these _____ in the computer lab: No eating or drinking.
3. There are ten students, but only five books. Please _____ a book with a partner.
4. Connie has a _____ room at the hospital. She is the only person in the room.
5. Pedro lives in a two-bedroom apartment. He has a _____ named Bill.
6. Yuriko is living with a _____ in London. The daughter is the same age as Yuriko.

C Pair work. Imagine you and your partner are students at Madison.
Which housing do you like? Answer the questions.

Do you want to live ☐ with a host family? ☐ in a dorm room? Why?

In the dorm, do you want ☐ a private room? ☐ a double room with a roommate? Why?

A Listen. Complete the sentence. (CD 2, Track 33)

Graciela is having a problem with her roommate / schoolwork / housing.

  B Listen again. Where does Graciela live now?
Circle the letter. (CD 2, Track 34)

  C Pair work. Listen one last time. Graciela wants to change her housing.
Why? Tell your partner. (CD 2, Track 35)

3 Reading

Make yourself at home!

> At your house, do you make your own breakfast or dinner? clean? do your own laundry?

A Read the journal entry on page 111. Then choose a title for the entry. Write your
answer at the top of the entry.

  a. My Family in Taipei
  b. My College Roommate
  c. My Host Family in America

B Read the journal again. Circle *True* or *False* for each sentence.
Change the false sentences to make them true.

1. Yaopeng shares a room with Jason.	True	False
2. Yaopeng's host mother is married with two children.	True	False
3. Patricia doesn't clean, cook, or do laundry for Yaopeng.	True	False
4. Yaopeng's friends usually visit the apartment on Mondays or Tuesdays.	True	False
5. On the weekend, Jason watches videos with his friends in the living room.	True	False

_____, Yaopeng Wong

July 2004
Denver, Colorado, U.S.A.

This is my third month as a student in Denver, Colorado. I'm learning a lot in English class. I'm writing in this journal to practice my English.

I'm living with a host family. Patricia, my host mother, is really nice. She's divorced and has two kids — a seventeen-year-old son, Jason, and a twelve-year-old daughter, Clarissa. We live in a large apartment. I have my own room. It has a bed, a desk, and a small closet. We share the bathroom and a computer in the living room. I can also use the kitchen or watch TV in the living room.

Living with an American family is interesting. On the first day here, Patricia showed me the house and my room. She said, "Make yourself at home." At first, I didn't understand, but now I do. The house is like my house. I usually make breakfast for myself. I do my own laundry. I clean my own room. Patricia is my host mother, but she is like a friend or a roommate. But, there are rules. It's okay for my friends to visit, but only on the weekend. Jason's friends come to the apartment on the weekend. They hang out in his room and listen to music or watch videos. Sometimes my friends from school have dinner with my family.

Me in Denver

ask&
ANSWER
What does the expression *Make yourself at home* mean? Is there a similar expression in your language? Think about Yaopeng's host family. Is your house and family similar or different? How?

> Many verbs in English are followed by a preposition. Some prepositions are *at, about, for, to, with*.

verb	prep.	noun		verb	prep.	noun phrase
Jason listens	to	music.		I listen	to	the radio.

A Underline the verb + preposition in each sentence.

1. Let's not take a taxi. Let's <u>wait for</u> the bus.
2. Tom is talking to his roommate, Sean.
3. Joey is talking about his roommate, Lance.
4. Robert is looking at the menu.
5. Yoshi is looking for his keys.
6. Mona lives with her grandmother.

B Match each picture with a sentence from A.

C Complete the sentences with a verb + preposition from A.
Use the correct form of the verb.

1. A: Sheila, who are you __talking to__ ?
   B: Ellen. We're _____ our trip to Las Vegas.

2. A: What are you _____?
   B: My sunglasses. I lost them!

3. A: Do you want to _____ a taxi?
   B: No, let's walk.

4. A: Why are you _____ that woman?
   B: I think I know her.

5. I _____ my family in a large apartment.

5 Writing

My house

A Read the description of an apartment in Hong Kong. Then write about your house or apartment.

I live with my family in an apartment in Hong Kong. We live on the sixteenth floor. There are two bedrooms, a living room, a kitchen, a bathroom, and a balcony. There are plants on the balcony. The balcony has big glass doors. I share a bedroom with my sister. In the room, there are two beds. There is also a desk, a closet, and a stereo. We like to listen to music at night before we go to sleep. Sometimes, we talk about our day.

B Pair work. Share your writing with a partner. Ask questions about your partner's house or apartment.

6 Communication

Looking for a roommate

A Read the advertisement and answer the questions.

1. How many rooms are there in the apartment?
2. Is there a private room for you? What rooms do you share?
3. Where is the apartment?
4. What are the house rules?

B Imagine you have an apartment. You want a roommate. Write an ad on a separate piece of paper.

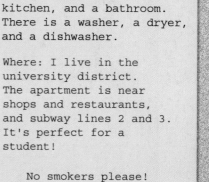

Looking for a roommate!

Share a large, five-room apartment with me. There are two bedrooms, a kitchen, and a bathroom. There is a washer, a dryer, and a dishwasher.

Where: I live in the university district. The apartment is near shops and restaurants, and subway lines 2 and 3. It's perfect for a student!

No smokers please!

C Group work. Work with a group of 3 or 4 people. Tell them about your apartment. Your group asks questions about your apartment.

Is there a washer and dryer?

Is the apartment near shops?

What are your house rules?

 Check out the World Link video. **Practice your English online at** http://elt.thomson.com/worldlink

1 Vocabulary Link

What are you wearing?

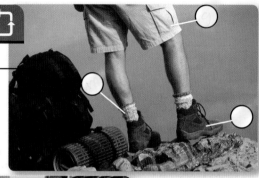

A Match each word with an item in the pictures.

CLOTHES

a. dress

b. coat

c. jacket

d. suit

e. (a pair of) pants

f. (a pair of) jeans

g. (a pair of) shorts

h. skirt

i. blouse

j. T-shirt

k. sweater

l. tie

m. (a pair of) socks

SHOES

n. (a pair of) boots

o. (a pair of) sandals

p. (a pair of) sneakers

q. (a pair of) heels

She's wearing a dress and heels.

B Pair work. Look at the photos again. What is each person wearing? Tell a partner.

ask&
ANSWER

1. Look at the photos. What clothes are for men? for women? for both?
2. What are you wearing now? Tell your partner.
3. What clothes do you wear in the summer? the winter? the spring? the fall?

2 Listening

Window shopping

 A Tina and Luke are window shopping. Listen.
Write 1, 2, or 3 next to the windows. One is extra. (CD 2, Track 36)

 B Listen again. What store do Tina and Luke go in? Circle it. (CD 2, Track 37)

 C Listen again. Circle the best answer to complete each sentence. (CD 2, Track 38)

1. Tina likes / doesn't like the sweater.
2. She likes / doesn't like the sandals.

3. She is / isn't looking for summer clothes.
4. It is / isn't her brother's birthday soon.

ask&
ANSWER
Where is a good area for window shopping in your city?

 **World Link**

In Tibet, it's against the law to wear white shoes.

Source: Ripley's Believe It or Not!

3 Pronunciation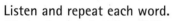

Vowel sounds

 A Listen and repeat each word.
Circle the word with a different vowel sound. (CD 2, Track 39)

1. jeans   heels   green   slip
2. his   he's   million   with
3. tie   high   white   wish

 B Pair work. Say the words below with your partner.
Then put them in the correct row in A (1, 2, or 3).

sleeve   buy   window   sneakers   fifty   clip   light

 C Listen and check your answers. (CD 2, Track 40)

How much is the red coat?

A Pair work. **Listen to the conversation. Then practice with a partner. One partner plays Luke *and* the clerk.**
(CD 2, Track 41)

Luke:	Hey, Tina. Look at that coat in the window.
Tina:	Oh, it's cool. How much is it?
Luke:	I don't know. I don't see a price.
	Let's go in the store and ask.
Tina:	Excuse me.
Clerk:	Yes?
Tina:	How much is the red coat?
Clerk:	The red coat? It's a hundred dollars.

B Pair work. **Use the pictures and the Useful Expressions to make new conversations. Practice with your partner.**

$200

$75

$60

$55

Useful Expressions:
Asking for and giving prices

How much is the red coat?	(It's) $200.
How much is it?	(two hundred dollars)
How much are these gray pants?	They are $25.
How much are they?	(twenty-five dollars)

Colors

● black   ● orange
● blue   ● pink
● brown   ● purple
● dark blue   ● red
● green   ○ white
● gray   ○ yellow
○ light blue

ask & ANSWER

What's your favorite color?
Think about the clothes and shoes in your closet.
What colors are they? Where do you buy your clothes?

5 Language Link

Numbers 100 to 50,000

one = a
one hundred = a hundred

100	one hundred	1,000	one thousand	10,000	ten thousand
120	one hundred (and) twenty	1,200	one thousand two hundred twelve hundred	12,000	twelve thousand
155	one hundred (and) fifty-five	1,550	one thousand five hundred (and) fifty	15,550	fifteen thousand five hundred (and) fifty
500	five hundred	5,000	five thousand	50,000	fifty thousand

A Pair work. Say the numbers below. Use the chart to help you.

108   305   450   1,200   3,425   6,000   11,000   15,500   25,000   45,375

B Pair work. Think of five numbers. Say them to your partner.
Your partner writes them.

US $	¥
45	5,400
105	12,339
110	12,926
120	14,100
250	29,950
315	37,700

C Hiroko is from Japan. She is shopping on the Internet.
The store's prices are in U.S. dollars only. She has 50,000 yen ($425).
Help Hiroko choose two things.

JOJO's FASHION ONLINE

View Others   My Shopping Cart   Search: [   ] GO   JOJO's

VIEW ITEM   VIEW ITEM   VIEW ITEM   VIEW ITEM   VIEW ITEM

Leather Jacket $315   *Earrings* $110   *Skirt* $105   *Sweater* $250   *Blouse* $45

D Pair work. Tell your partner your choices.
Say the prices in dollars and yen.

I like the blouse. It's 45 dollars. That's 5,400 yen.

 ask & ANSWER
Do you shop on the Internet? What do you buy?
Dollars are used in the United States. Yen are used in Japan.
What money is used in the U.K.? Mexico? Italy? Australia?

It's a bargain!

 Pair work. Practice the conversation with a partner.
Then answer the questions.

Clerk:	Can I help you?
Customer:	Yes, I'm looking for a leather jacket.
Clerk:	I have a brown leather jacket. It's from Italy.
Customer:	Oh, it's beautiful! How much is it?
Clerk:	$300.
Customer:	$300?! That's very expensive.
Clerk:	Okay, for you, $250.
Customer:	$200.
Clerk:	$225.
Customer:	Okay, I'll take it!

1. The man wants to buy a leather jacket. At the beginning, how much is the jacket?
2. How much is the jacket at the end?

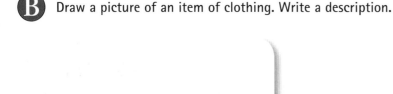 Draw a picture of an item of clothing. Write a description.

_____

black leather boots

 Pair work. Work with a partner. Take turns selling your items to each other. Bargain for a price! Write down the price your partner paid in the chart below.

 Class activity. Now sell the same item to two more classmates. Write down the price each person pays. At the end, tell the class how much money you have.

Customer's name		Price
1. _____		_____
2. _____	+	_____
3. _____	+	_____
	=	_____

Clothing

Lesson B | What do I wear?

1 Vocabulary Link

Spring sale

A Look at the website. Match a word with an item in the website.

> **a.** ring   **c.** bracelet   **e.** hat   **g.** long *(adj.)*
> **b.** necklace **d.** earrings   **f.** sunglasses   **h.** short *(adj.)*

B Class activity. Discuss these questions with your classmates.

1. Do you like to wear jewelry, sunglasses, or hats?
2. What styles of clothing are popular these days?
3. What kinds of clothes do you like to wear?

2 Listening

Store sales

 A Listen to the radio advertisements.
Write the name of the company in the correct box. (CD 2, Track 42)

- The Far Company   • Byron's Department Store

Prices: Start at $ _____
Sale: Buy _____ items and
you get _____ for free.

Prices: $ _____ to $ _____
Sale: Get a free _____ when
you spend $ _____ or more.

 B Listen again. Write the prices at each store. (CD 2, Track 43)

 C Listen again. The stores are having a sale.
Complete the sentences about each sale. (CD 2, Track 44)

ask&
ANSWER

What stores often have sales?
When do stores usually have sales?
Some people like to shop at sales. Do you?

 World Link

When she died in 1762,
Elizabeth I of Russia had
thousands of pairs of shoes.
She also had more than
15,000 dresses!

3 Reading

Ask Amanda

Imagine this: An American friend invites you to a dinner party at her house.
What clothes will you wear? Complete this sentence: I will wear _____.

 A Pair work. Read the letter to Amanda on page 121. Don't read Amanda's reply!
Choose the answer you think is correct. Explain your answer to a partner.

1. Wear formal clothes to the party. Bring an expensive gift.
2. Wear casual clothes to the party. Bring a small gift.

Jeans are *casual*.
A suit is *formal*.

B Now read Amanda's answer.
Was your answer in A correct? Tell your partner.

Ask Amanda

Do you have a question about travel or living in another country? Write to Amanda. She can help you!

Dear Amanda,

I'm from Thailand, and I'm a graduate student in Dallas, Texas. I have a night class on Thursday. The professor (an American) invited the class to visit his home this Saturday for a dinner party. It's his birthday. I'm learning a lot about American customs, but I'm not sure about two things: What do I wear to the party? Also, do I give my professor a gift?

Thanks for your help.
Susan Jala

Dear Susan,

A birthday party is usually an informal event. For your professor's birthday dinner, wear something casual, but nice. Don't wear a formal dress or suit. Americans of all ages often wear casual clothes—especially outside the workplace.

About the gift—yes, it's common to give a birthday present. Give your professor something small—for example, a book or a box of candy. Don't give personal gifts like clothing or jewelry.

Enjoy the party!
Amanda

C Read the sentences. Circle the correct answer.

1. Susan is from the U.S. / Thailand.
2. Susan's teacher / friend asked her to a party at his house / the university.
3. Amanda tells Susan to wear / not to wear a formal dress to the party.
4. In the U.S., people usually / hardly ever wear casual clothes outside the workplace.
5. A watch / nice box of candy is a good gift for Susan's professor.

ask & ANSWER

Do you go to parties often? What do you usually wear?
Describe a really fun party.

4 Language Link

Count and noncount nouns

In English, there are **count nouns** and **noncount nouns**.

Count nouns		Noncount nouns
singular	plural	
an earring	two earrings	jewelry
a ring	three rings	money _____
a/an _____	four _____	_____
a/an _____	two _____	_____
a/an _____	three _____	_____
a/an _____	four _____	_____
a/an _____	two _____	_____
a/an _____	three _____	

A Write the nouns below in the chart above. Write both the singular and the plural forms of the count nouns.

~~money~~	shirt	soup	math	page	chair
dollar	clothing	banana	homework	book	furniture

B Complete the sentences with *is* or *are*.

1. There _____ furniture in this room.
2. History _____ my favorite subject.
3. _____ clothing expensive in your country?
4. There _____ four chairs in the kitchen.
5. Here _____ a dollar for the bus.

6. The money _____ on the table.
7. There _____ seven days in a week.
8. This homework _____ very hard.
9. Be careful! The soup _____ hot.
10. Are you hungry? There _____ bananas in the kitchen.

5 Writing

What are you wearing?

A On a separate piece of paper, write about the things you are wearing.

Describe . . .
- your clothes and their colors and style
- other things you are wearing—jewelry, glasses, a hat

B Give your paper to your teacher. Your teacher gives you another student's paper. Read it. Who is the writer?

I'm wearing a pair of blue jeans, a gray T-shirt, a dark blue jacket, and a blue hat. My socks are white and my boots are black. I'm wearing jewelry.

6 Communication

Answer and win!

 A Read the directions.

1. Get into groups of three or four. One person is the game host. The others close their books.
2. Player 1 chooses a category: Clothing and jewelry, Money and numbers, or Colors. The game host reads the first question in that category.
3. If Player 1 answers correctly, he or she gets the points.
4. The game continues with the next player. Repeat steps 2 and 3.
5. The winner is the student with the most points.

> I choose "Color."

> For 100 points—what are the colors of your country's flag?

 B For 300 extra points: At the end, find two count nouns and two noncount nouns in the three boxes.

Clothing and jewelry

100: Name three things a partner is wearing.
200: Complete the movie title: *Lord of the* _____.
300: Name one kind of clothing for women only.
400: Choose the correct answer: Jeans are a kind of formal / casual clothing.
500: Which is *not* a kind of jewelry: a necklace / a bracelet / a hat?
600: Complete the sentence: A person with pierced *ears* wears _____.
700: Name a traditional item of clothing in Japan.
800: Name a clothing designer.

Money and numbers

100: What is 1,000 + 500?
200: How much is a bus ride in your city?
300: What is 1,200 + 10,500?
400: What money is used in many countries in Europe?
500: How many zeros are there in the number ten thousand?
600: What is 2,300 - 200?
700: What money is used in Canada?
800: What does *I'm broke* mean? Does it mean *I don't have any money* OR *I have money*?

Colors

100: What are the colors of your country's flag?
200: This color means "stop."
300: The president of the United States lives in the _____ House.
400: What color is paper money in the U.S.A.?
500: This color is also the name of a fruit.
600: In the 1930s, many movies were not in color. The movies were in _____ and white.
700: The Beatles have a famous song called "_____ Submarine."
800: What does *I'm blue* mean? Does it mean *I'm happy, I'm sad,* or *I'm angry*?

> Check your answers on page 154.

 Check out the World Link video. **Practice your English online at** http://elt.thomson.com/worldlink

1 Vocabulary Link

What do you do?

J.K. Rowling is a writer.

A Do you know these people?
Match a job with a person.

a. ~~writer~~
b. singer
c. actor
d. fashion designer
e. painter
f. race-car driver
g. dancer
h. inventor

J.K. Rowling

Alexander Graham Bell

Michael Flatley

Ayrton Senna

Frida Kahlo

Shakira

Will Smith

Jean Paul Gaultier

B Match each job with a person.

a. receptionist
b. nurse
c. doctor
d. businesswoman
e. dentist
f. waitress

2 Listening

A part-time job

A Listen to Ramón and Lisa talking about jobs. Number the pictures from 1 to 4 as you listen. (CD 2, Track 45)

ALL IN A DAY'S WORK

Job Title: _____

Days: _____

Hours: _____

Job Title: _____

Days: _____

Hours: _____

Job Title: _____

Days: _____

Hours: _____

Job Title: _____'s assistant

Days: _____

Hours: _____

B Listen again. Complete the chart above. (CD 2, Track 46)

World Link

The average U.S. worker has more than nine jobs in his or her lifetime.

Source: *U.S. Department of Labor*

3 Pronunciation

Reduced *What do you* and *What does*

A Listen and repeat. Pay attention to the reduced pronunciation of *What do you* and *What does*. (CD 2, Track 47)

What do you do?   What does she do?   What does he do?

B Listen to the questions. Then circle the correct answers. (CD 2, Track 48)

1. a. He studies English.   b. I study music.
2. a. She's a chef.   b. He's a receptionist.
3. a. I want a cold drink.   b. She wants to leave.
4. a. He's a musician.   b. She's a businesswoman.
5. a. I want to be rich!   b. He wants a good job.
6. a. I think Mary is friendly.   b. He thinks Mary is friendly.

> *What do you want to be?*

C Pair work. Choose four answers in B, but don't tell your partner. Now say a question for each answer. Your partner must find the correct answer.

> *I want to be rich!*

A Listen to the conversation between two people at Ramón's birthday party. Underline the jobs. (CD 2, Track 49)

Lisa:	Hi, are you a friend of Ramón's?
Brad:	Yeah, my name is Brad.
Lisa:	Hi, Brad. I'm Lisa. Are you a university student?
Brad:	No, I'm a nurse.
Lisa:	Oh? That's interesting.
Brad:	What do you do, Lisa?
Lisa:	I'm a university student now. I want to be a high school teacher. I also have a part-time job.
Brad:	Where do you work?
Lisa:	I'm a waitress at a café.
Brad:	Wow, you're really hardworking!

 B Pair work. Practice the conversation with a partner.

 C Role play.
Imagine you are guests at Ramón's party. Create and act out two conversations like the one in A.

Conversation 1

Student A:	**Todd**
	newspaper reporter

Student B:	**Carmen**
	student
	wants to be: a nurse
	part-time job: a receptionist

Conversation 2

Student A:	**Rick**
	writer

Student B:	**Sally**
	student
	wants to be: a dance instructor
	part-time job: a cashier

> **Useful Expressions:**
> **Asking about jobs**
>
> What do you do?
> I'm a *student*.
> I'm an *actress*.
> I'm *self-employed*.
>
> What do you want to be?
> *A teacher*.

 D Group work. Interview three classmates. Complete the chart.

What do you want to be?

What do you do?

A high school teacher.

I'm a student and a waitress.

name	present job(s)	wants to be . . .
Lisa	a student and a waitress at a café	a high school teacher
1.		
2.		
3.		

Personality adjectives

A Answer the question for each picture. Use words from the box.

hardworking	lazy	funny	serious
outgoing	shy	smart	creative

What's Lisa like?
She's hardworking .

What's Mrs. Simmons like?
_____.

What's Peter like?
_____.

What's Olivia like?
_____.

What are Yoshi's
classmates like?
_____.

What's Mauricio's sister like?
_____.

What's Fernando like?
_____.

What are Lisa's parents like?
_____.

B Which adjectives above are positive? Which are negative? Which are both? Write them in the chart.

Positive	Negative	Both
hardworking		

C Do you know other personality adjectives? Add them to the chart in B. Tell the class.

ask & ANSWER

What are you like?	What are your parents like?
What is your best friend like?	What are your classmates like?
What is your _____ like?	What are your _____ like?

Here's my card

 A Pair work. Look at the business cards. What information do you see? Tell a partner.

> *Elena Perez's card has her name and job title. It also has . . .*

EH

The Embassy Hotel

Sean Curtis
General Manager

390 Post Street
San Francisco, CA 90080
Tel: (415) 555-9090, extension 245
www.EmbassyHotel.net

Que Colores QC

Elena Perez Ramirez
Artist

Princesa 25 8-8
28003 Madrid
Tel: 91 555 53 26
elenapr@quecolores.es

B Pair work. Look at the answers. Write the questions. Check answers with a partner.

1. _____? My name is Elena Perez.
2. _____? I'm an artist. I teach children to draw.
3. _____? I'm from Madrid, Spain.
4. _____? I work at an art school, Que Colores.
5. _____? My e-mail address is elenapr@quecolores.es.
6. _____? My coworkers are very friendly.
7. _____? Yes, I like my job a lot!

C Think of your dream job. On three pieces of paper, make three copies of your business card.

D Class activity. Imagine you are at a party. Introduce yourself to three people. Give each person your business card. Ask and answer the questions in B.

E Class activity. Tell your class about one person at the party. What was the person like?

ask**&**
ANSWER

Do your friends or family members usually talk about their jobs?
What are some unusual jobs for women?
What are some unusual jobs for men?

Jobs and Ambitions

Lesson B | Getting a job

1 Vocabulary Link

Help wanted

 A Read the want ads. Pay attention to the words in blue.

> ## Wanted: Part-time **Translator**
>
> We need a person to translate e-mail and faxes from Spanish to English. Salary: $10,000 a year. Please speak and write English and Spanish fluently.

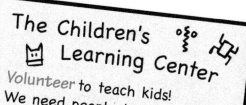

The Children's Learning Center
Volunteer to teach kids! We need people to teach basic computer skills—Microsoft Word® and e-mail. No pay, but we give free lunches.

B What parts of speech are the words in blue?
Write them in the chart.

noun	verb	adverb
1. _____	4. _____	6. fluently
2. _____	5. _____	
3. _____		

C Pair work. Denise is interviewing Carlos for a job at *La Vida* magazine.
Complete the interview with the words from A. Then practice the dialog with a partner.

Denise: So, Carlos, we want to _____translate_____ our online magazine from Spanish to English.

Carlos: Well, I speak and write both languages _____.

Denise: That's great. Are you working as a _____ now?

Carlos: Yes. At my university, I _____ at the school newspaper. I work in English and Spanish.

Denise: Great. Tell me about your computer _____.

Carlos: Well, I can use a PC and a Macintosh. I can also build websites.

Denise: Perfect! This job is 20 hours a week. The _____ is $15,000 a year.

Carlos: Sounds good to me!

 ask & ANSWER

> Where do people find jobs? On the Internet? In newspaper want ads? At school? When do people usually start working? For college students, is it easy to find jobs?

2 Listening

Job advertisements

  A Listen. Number the job advertisements (1, 2, 3) in the order you hear. (CD 2, Track 50)

JOBS
Computer games tester needed. Work at home!
Skills: _____
Pay: _____ an hour ☐

JOBS
Music teacher for elementary school
Skills: _____
Pay: _____ an hour ☐

JOBS
PAY: $30,000 a year
International Flight Attendant
Skills: _____ ☐

  B Listen again. Complete each want ad. (CD 2, Track 51)

ask &
ANSWER
Which job do you like? Why?

World Link

In British English, most people refer to a resume as a "CV" (curriculum vitae). A CV is usually longer and more detailed.

3 Reading

My resume

A *resume* is a page or two of information about you. In many countries, you give your resume to a company you want to work for. What kind of information is on a resume?

A Read the resume on page 131. What job is right for Anthony Price? Circle it.

THE PAPER — Classified Jobs

Chefs needed for popular Japanese restaurant!

Call now to arrange for interview: (617) 555-7965

WANTED
JAPANESE/ ENGLISH TRANSLATOR
781-555-8000

Graphic Artist.
Send your résumé to the University of Chicago, Department of East Asian Studies.
E-mail: work@uoc.edu.net

B Read the resume again. Then answer the questions.

Anthony Price
4471 25th Street
Irvine, CA 95432 U.S.A.
Tel.: (209) 555-4432 e-mail: tonyp@bestjobs.com

EDUCATION

University of Chicago, Chicago, IL
Bachelor of Arts, East Asian Studies   May 2004
Activities: Japanese Club president from 2003-2004

Waseda University, Tokyo, Japan
Studied Japanese language, history, and culture
                                                            Aug. 2002–May 2003

WORK EXPERIENCE

WebTrans: A translation company, Chicago, IL
Part-time Translator   Aug. 2004–present
Translate websites from English to Japanese.

One World Travel Magazine, Boston, MA
Part-time Travel Writer   Aug. 2004–present
Research and write articles about different U.S. cities.

Museum of Modern Art, Chicago, IL
Volunteer Teacher   May 2004–present
Teach a 30-minute class – "The Art of Japan" – once a week.

The Pacific Market, Chicago, IL
Cashier   Nov. 2000–May 2002

LANGUAGES
Can speak, read, and write Japanese and English fluently.

COMPUTER SKILLS
Microsoft Word®, Excel®, and DreamWeaver®
Can use both a PC and a Macintosh.

C Read the sentences. Circle *True* or *False*.
Change the false sentences to make them true.

1. Anthony lives in Japan now.	True	False
2. Right now, Anthony has two full-time jobs.	True	False
3. Anthony speaks two languages very well.	True	False
4. Anthony writes articles for a travel magazine.	True	False
5. Anthony makes $20 an hour at the Museum of Modern Art.	True	False
6. Anthony can use a PC only.	True	False

ask**&**
ANSWER
Look again at Anthony's resume. What things can he do? What jobs can he get with these skills? Explain your ideas. To get a job today, which skills are important?

Talking about abilities: *can* and *can't*

 A Read the questions and answers in the chart.
Pay attention to the use of *can* and *can't*.

Can you speak French?	Yes, I can. No, I can't.
Which languages can you speak?	(I can speak) Spanish.

B Pair work. Is your partner a good person for the tour guide job?
Read the ad. Write 3 *yes/no* questions with *can*. Then ask your partner.

1. <u>Can you work in Bali this summer</u> ?
2. _____ ?
3. _____ ?
4. _____ ?

> Can you work in Bali this summer?

> Yes, I can.

WANTED: Tour guide

Vacation hotel in beautiful Bali needs a hardworking, friendly tour guide this summer.

Your duties: lead groups of people to areas of interest around the island.

Skills needed: Please . . .
speak English and one other language.
swim well.
drive a car.

Send your resume to bobby@balivac.org

 C Pair work. Look at Adam's and Sonya's information.
Make questions with *can* using the words.

Adam Schmidt: Musician/guitar player
Languages: English and German
Hobbies: I like to ski and swim.

Sonya Delgado: Webmaster
Languages: Spanish and English
Hobbies: I like to dance and ski.

1. Who/speak German? <u>Who can speak German</u> ?
2. What/languages/Sonya/speak? _____ ?
3. Who/build/websites? _____ ?
4. What/instrument/Adam/play? _____ ?
5. Who/ski? _____ ?

D Pair work. Take turns asking and answering the questions in C with a partner.

> Who can speak German?

> Adam can.

5 Writing

What can you do?

 Read about this student's skills.
Then write about three skills you have.

 Pair work. Exchange your writing with
a partner. Read about your partner's
skills. Tell the class about your partner.

*I have three important skills.
First, I can play two instruments.
I can play the guitar and the piano.
On the weekend, I meet my friends
and we play music together. We
have a band called Los Amantes
(The Lovers). In my band, I play
guitar and I am also the singer. I
can read music, but I can't write
it. In the future, I want to be a
music teacher, or maybe a famous
musician!*

6 Communication

The right job

 Read the questions in the chart.
Think about your answers.

 Pair work. Ask a partner the questions in the chart. Use *can*. For your partner's answers, write a number:

3 = Yes, I can. 2 = Yes, a little bit. 1 = No, I can't.

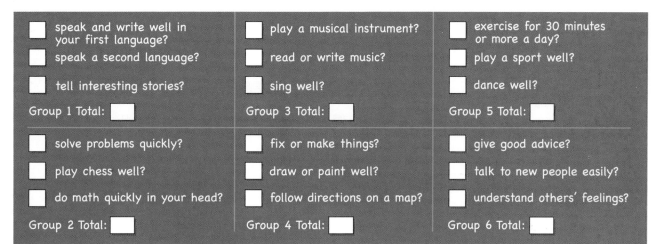

☐ speak and write well in your first language?	☐ play a musical instrument?	☐ exercise for 30 minutes or more a day?
☐ speak a second language?	☐ read or write music?	☐ play a sport well?
☐ tell interesting stories?	☐ sing well?	☐ dance well?
Group 1 Total: ☐	Group 3 Total: ☐	Group 5 Total: ☐
☐ solve problems quickly?	☐ fix or make things?	☐ give good advice?
☐ play chess well?	☐ draw or paint well?	☐ talk to new people easily?
☐ do math quickly in your head?	☐ follow directions on a map?	☐ understand others' feelings?
Group 2 Total: ☐	Group 4 Total: ☐	Group 6 Total: ☐

C Now add the points for each group and write the totals.
Then look at the chart below. What are good jobs for your partner?

7-9 points in...	Good jobs for you:
Group 1	teacher, lawyer, salesperson, actor
Group 2	businessperson, computer programmer, doctor
Group 3	musician, DJ, singer

7-9 points in...	Good jobs for you:
Group 4	graphic artist, fashion designer, photographer, engineer
Group 5	dancer, athlete, fitness instructor
Group 6	teacher, manager, salesperson

D Pair work. Look again at the chart in B.
When did your partner say, "Yes, I can"?
Ask your partner questions about these abilities.

Can you speak a second language?

Yes, I can.

What language can you speak?

I can speak Spanish.

 Check out the World Link video.

 Practice your English online at http://elt.thomson.com/worldlink

1 Storyboard

 A Pair work. Gary and Mina are at a party. Sabrina and Joey are shopping in Mexico City. Complete the two conversations.

Conversation 1: Gary and Mina

_____?

That's Luis. He's my _____.
We share an apartment near school.

What _____?

He's a really nice guy.

What _____?

He's a student.

Conversation 2: Sabrina and Joey

REBAJAS de VERANO

Hey, I don't speak Spanish. _____ the sign?

Yes, _____. It says "Summer Sale!" Let's go inside.

This is a nice jacket. How _____?

It's 570 pesos.

_____ it in U.S. dollars?

It's about 50 dollars.

B Pair work. Practice the conversations.

C Pair work. Change roles and practice again.

2 See it and say it

 A This store sells many things. Write the word on the correct sign in the picture below.

    Furniture   Clothing   Jewelry   Appliances

B Pair work. Study the picture.
Take turns answering the questions with a partner.

1. What things are in each section of the store?
2. How many rugs are there in the store? Lamps? Sales clerks? Chairs? Windows? Tables? Mirrors?
3. Look at the people in the picture. What are they wearing?

C Pair work. Four pairs of people are talking.
What are they saying? Role-play four short conversations.

Excuse me. How much is that watch?

It's . . .

3 Spot the differences

A Look at the two pictures. Where are these people? What are they doing?

B Pair work. Find the differences with a partner. How many do you see?

4 Want ads

A Pair work. Look at the want ads. Can you do these jobs? Explain to your partner.

> *I can do the receptionist job.*
> *I can type quickly and ...*

THE PAPER   Classified Jobs

Sundance Studio needs a dance teacher!

Teach adults and children to dance
You: Friendly and creative dance teacher.
Work well with children ages 6-8.
Days and hours: Thursday, Friday, Saturday
                    5:00-10:00 PM

Pay: $35 per hour
Call 487-9888 for interview now!

Wanted: Friendly, hardworking receptionist for an international office

You: Type quickly
Speak English and one of these languages:
Korean, Spanish, Japanese, Chinese, Portuguese
Days and hours: Monday – Friday 8 a.m. – 5 p.m.
Salary: $28,000 per year
CALL (789) 089-0899

B Think of a job and make a want ad on a separate piece of paper. Write the job, the days and hours, the pay, and the skills needed.

C Class activity. Put your ad on the classroom wall. Read the other ads. Which jobs can you do? Make a list on a piece of paper.

D Pair work. Tell a partner about the jobs on your list. Which job do you want?

5 Listening: Winchester Mystery House

A Class activity. **Look at the pictures of this famous house.**
Use three adjectives to describe the house. Share your ideas with the class.

a staircase inside the house   a door inside the house   a door outside the house

 B Listen to a tour guide talk about the Winchester Mystery House. (CD 2, Track 52)

 C Listen again. Write the numbers. (CD 2, Track 53)

total rooms	bedrooms	bathrooms	elevators	doors	windows	staircases	kitchens

 D Pair work. **Answer the questions with a partner.**

1. Why is this house strange? Choose one example from the talk.
2. Some people think the house is haunted. Do you know a haunted house? Tell your partner about it.

Language Summaries

Unit 1 Greetings and Intros

Lesson A

Vocabulary Link

e-mail address
female
first name
last name
male
nickname
numbers 0–10
phone number
spelling
student
teacher

Language Link

Subject pronouns
Possessive adjectives

Speaking

**Useful Expressions:
Introducing yourself**

Hi, what's your name?
   My name is Mariko.
I'm Mariko.
   I'm Frank Whitman.
My name is Sally Kim.
    (It's) nice to meet you.
    (It's) nice to meet you, too.

Lesson B

Vocabulary Link

actor
boyfriend
classmate
family
famous
favorite
friend
girlfriend
golfer
martial artist
singer
soccer player

Language Link

Yes/No questions and short
answers with *be*

Unit 2 Countries and Nationalities

Lesson A

Vocabulary Link

city
country
nationality
vacation

Brazil/Brazilian
China/Chinese
France/French
Japan/Japanese
Korea/Korean
Mexico/Mexican
The U.K./British
The U.S./American

Language Link

Question words:
where and *who*

Speaking

**Useful Expressions:
Asking where someone
is from**

Where are you from?
   I'm from Mexico.
Where is he from?
   He's from Korea.
Are you from Mexico?
   Yes, I am.
   No, I'm not. I'm from Peru.
Which city are you from?
   I'm from Vancouver.

Lesson B

Vocabulary Link

beautiful
big
boring
cheap
clean
crowded
dirty
empty
expensive
interesting
modern
noisy
old
quiet
small
ugly

Language Link

Be + adjective

Unit 3 *Interesting Products*

Lesson A

Vocabulary Link

answering machine
camera
CD player
cell phone
key
laptop (computer)
purse
watch

Language Link

Plurals; *this/that/these/those*

Speaking

**Useful Expressions:
Saying *Thank you***

Thank you so much.
Thank you.
Thanks a lot.
Thanks.

Replies

You're welcome
My pleasure.
Sure, no problem.

Lesson B

Vocabulary Link

camcorder
DVD player
MP3 player
stereo
TV
VCR

compact
heavy
inexpensive
lightweight
new

Language Link

Adjectives and nouns

Unit 4 *Activities and Interests*

Lesson A

Vocabulary Link

cooking
eating
exercising
listening to music
playing the guitar
reading
singing
sleeping
studying
watching TV

Language Link

The present continuous

Speaking

**Useful Expressions:
Asking how someone is (1)**

How are you doing?
  (I'm) fine.
      all right.
      okay.
      so-so.

How about you?

Lesson B

Vocabulary Link

art
art history
business
cooking
English
history
literature
math
music
science
writing
yoga

Language Link

The present continuous:
extended time

Language Summaries

Unit 5 Food

Lesson A

Vocabulary Link

bacon and eggs
bottled water
breakfast
cereal
chicken
chicken sandwich
chocolate cake
coffee
desserts
dinner
drinks
fish
garlic
ice cream
lunch
pasta
pizza
soda
soup and salad
steak
tea
tomatoes

Language Link

The simple present

Speaking

**Useful Expressions:
Talking about likes and dislikes**

Do you like Italian food?
Do you like fish?
  Yes! I love it!
  Yes, I like it a lot.
  Yes, it's okay.
  No, I don't really like it.
  No, I can't stand it.

Lesson B

Vocabulary Link

clothes
festival
ice cream
noodles
pasta
sushi
traditional
visit

Language Link

The simple present: *Yes/No* questions and short answers

Unit 6 My Family

Lesson A

Vocabulary Link

brother
daughter
father
grandfather
grandmother
husband
mother
sister
son
wife

Language Link

Possessives

Speaking

**Useful Expressions:
Asking and answering
about family**

Do you have any brothers or sisters?
  Yes. I have a sister.
  Yes. I have an older brother.
  Yes. I have two brothers
    and one sister.
  No. I'm an only child.

Lesson B

Vocabulary Link

divorced
married
single
single parent
stepdaughter
stepfather

Language Link

Numbers 11 to 2,000

Unit 7 *Time*

Lesson A

Vocabulary Link

at night
in the afternoon
in the evening
in the morning
midnight
noon

two-oh-five/five past two
ten-ten/ten past ten
two-fifteen/a quarter past two
two-thirty/half past two
two forty-five/a quarter to three

Language Link

Prepositions of time: *in/on/at;*
question word *when*

Speaking

Useful Expressions:
Suggestions with *Let's*

Let's see the new *Star Wars* movie.
    Hmm . . . I don't really want
    to see that.

Then let's see *The Lord of the
Rings III.*
    Okay, that sounds good!

Lesson B

Vocabulary Link

go out with friends
go shopping
go to the movies
relax
spend time with family
take a trip somewhere
work
work out at the gym

Language Link

The simple present: *wh-* questions

Unit 8 *Special Occasions*

Lesson A

Vocabulary Link

January
February
March
April
May
June
July
August
September
October
November
December

Ordinal numbers

Language Link

Prepositions of time:
in and *on*

Speaking

Useful Expressions:
Saying you don't know

When is his birthday?
    I don't know. I think it's
    on the fourth.
How old is he?
    I'm not sure. I think he's 21.

Lesson B

Vocabulary Link

costume
deceased
decorate
New Year's Day
New Year's Eve
relative
remember
Valentine's Day

Language Link

How long; prepositions of time

Language Summaries

Unit 9 *Person to Person*

Lesson A

Vocabulary Link

check e-mail
do homework
get dressed
get home
get up
go to bed
go to school
take a shower
work

Language Link

Frequency adverbs

Speaking

Useful Expressions:
Asking how someone is (2)

How's it going?
   Great!
   Good.
   Not bad.
   Okay, I guess.
   So-so.
   Not so great.
   Don't ask!

Lesson B

Vocabulary Link

common
date (*n.*)
date (*v.*)
different
match
similar
split the bill

Language Link

Wh- questions about the subject

Unit 10 *Home Sweet Home*

Lesson A

Vocabulary Link

balcony
bathroom
bedroom
dining room
garage
kitchen
living room
yard

Language Link

There is/There are; How many

Speaking

Useful Expressions:
Showing surprise

Hey, this is a nice apartment!
   Thanks, and it's only $500
   a month.
Really? That's cheap!
Wow!
Oh?

Lesson B

Vocabulary Link

dormitory
host family
private
roommate
rules
share

Language Link

Verb + preposition

Unit 11 *Clothing*

Lesson A

Vocabulary Link

blouse
coat
dress
jacket
skirt
suit
sweater
tie
T-shirt
(a pair of) boots
(a pair of) heels
(a pair of) jeans
(a pair of) pants
(a pair of) sandals
(a pair of) shoes
(a pair of) shorts
(a pair of) sneakers
(a pair of) socks

Language Link

Numbers 100 to 50,000

Speaking

Useful Expressions:
Asking for and giving prices

How much is the red coat?
How much is it?
    (It's) $200.
        (two hundred dollars)
How much are these gray pants?
    They are $25.
        (twenty-five dollars)

Lesson B

Vocabulary Link

bracelet
earrings
hat
long (*adj.*)
necklace
ring
short (*adj.*)
sunglasses

Language Link

Count and noncount nouns

Unit 12 *Jobs and Ambitions*

Lesson A

Vocabulary Link

businessman/businesswoman
dancer
dentist
doctor
fashion designer
inventor
nurse
painter
race-car driver
receptionist
waiter/waitress
writer

Language Link

Personality adjectives

Speaking

Useful Expressions:
Asking about jobs

What do you do?
    I'm a student.
    I'm an actress.
    I'm self-employed
What do you want to be?
    A teacher.

Lesson B

Vocabulary Link

fluently
pay
salary
skills
translate
translator
volunteer

Language Link

Talking about abilities: *can* and *can't*

Grammar Notes

Unit 1 *Greetings and Intros*

Lesson A

Language Link: Subject pronouns and possessive adjectives with *be*

Subject pronouns + the verb *be*
I **am** a student.
You **are** a student.
She **is** a student.
He **is** a student.
The dog **is**/It **is** on the bed.

Possessive adjectives
My name is Mariko.
Your teacher is Emily.
Her name is Liujun.
His name is Paco.
Its name is Spot.

Lesson B

Language Link: *Yes/No* questions and short answers with *be*

Questions	Short Answers
Are you a student?	Yes, I am. No, I'm not.
Is he a student?	Yes, he is. No, he's not. No, he isn't.
Am I in this class?	Yes, you are. No, you're not. No, you aren't.
Is your name Sarah?	Yes, it is. No, it's not. No, it isn't.

Unit 2 *Countries and Nationalities*

Lesson A

Language Link: Question words *where* and *who*

Questions and answers with *who*

Questions	Answers
Who are you?	I'm Carmen.
Who is he?	He's my classmate. His name is Marco.
Who's she?	She's my teacher. Her name is Joanne.
Who is your classmate?	Marco is.
Who is from Mexico?	Marco is.

Questions and answers with *where*

Questions	Answers
Where are you from?	I'm from Seoul, Korea.
Where are you (now)?	I'm in the United States. I'm in New York City.
Where is Miami?	It's in the United States.
Where is the Eiffel Tower?	It's in Paris.

Lesson B

Language Link: *Be* + adjective

Paris is beautiful. Tokyo is safe.	An adjective can follow the verb *be*.
Paris is beautiful. Tokyo is safe. Paris is beautiful, and Tokyo is safe.	Use *and* to connect two sentences. Use a comma (,) before *and*.

Unit 3 *Interesting Products*

Lesson A

Language Link: Plurals; *this/that/these/those*

Singular nouns	Plural nouns
	(nouns + s)
an answering machine	two answering machines
a cell phone	three cell phones
a camera	four cameras
a book	five books
	(noun + es)
a watch	three watches
a dish	four dishes
a class	five classes
a box	six boxes
	(final y → ies)
a dictionary	two dictionaries
a city	three cities

Singular nouns	Plural nouns
	(irregular plurals)
a woman	two **women**
a man	three **men**
a person	four **people**
a child	five **children**
a sheep	two **sheep**
a deer	three **deer**
(no singular form)	eyeglasses
	clothes
	pants
	scissors

Grammar Notes

This/that/these/those

Use *this* to talk about a thing or person near you.	What's this? Who's this?	This is my cell phone. This is my classmate.
Use *that* to talk about a thing or person far from you.	What's that? Who's that?	That is my bike. That's my friend.
Use *these* to talk about two or more things or people near you	What are these? Who are these people?	These are my glasses. These are my classmates.
Use *those* to talk about two or more things or people far from you	What are those? Who are those people?	Those are my dictionaries. Those are my friends.

Plural subject pronouns and possessive adjectives

	Subject pronouns + *be*	Possessive adjectives
Frank and I are students. Mary and Sue are students.	We are students. They are students.	Our teacher is John. Their teacher is Emily.

Lesson B

Language Link: Adjectives and nouns

	be + adjective	Adjective + noun	
singular	This phone is expensive. This umbrella is beautiful.	This is an expensive phone. This is a beautiful umbrella.	Use *an* before adjectives or nouns that start with a vowel.
plural	These phones are expensive. These umbrellas are beautiful.	These are expensive cell phones. These are beautiful umbrellas.	Adjectives do not change form in the plural.

This is a **compact and lightweight cell phone.** This is a **compact, lightweight cell phone.**	Note: When 2 or more adjectives come before a noun, it is not always necessary to use *and*.

Unit 4 *Activities and Interests*

Lesson A

Language Link: The present continuous

The present continuous: subject + *be* + verb–*ing*

I am cooking. You are cooking. He is cooking. It is working. We are eating. They are talking. (negative forms) Anna is not dancing. They are not watching TV. They aren't watching TV.	If a verb ends in *e*, drop the *e* and then add –*ing*. dance → dancing make → making write → writing For a one-syllable verb ending in a consonant, double the last letter. Then add –*ing*. shop → shopping sit → sitting Words ending in *w, x,* or *y* do not double the last letter. He's playing guitar. She's fixing the radio.

The present continuous: *wh-* questions

What are you doing?	I'm cooking.
What is he doing?	He's reading.
What is he reading?	He's reading a magazine.
What are they doing?	They're watching TV.

The present continuous: *yes/no* questions and short answers

Are you listening to music?	Yes, I am. No, I'm not. I'm playing the guitar.
Are you eating dinner?	Yes, we are. No, we're not. We're watching TV.
Is John studying?	Yes, he is. No, he isn't. He's reading.
Are Tim and Mark playing basketball?	Yes, they are. No, they're not. They're playing a video game.

Grammar Notes

Lesson B

Language Link: Present continuous—extended time

actions happening right now	I'm **studying** for a test **right now**. Craig **is washing** the dishes. Simone **is sitting** on the floor.
actions happening these days	I'm **taking** three business classes **this semester**. Maria **is majoring** in English. I'm **meeting** a lot of people **these days**.

Other extended time expressions:
these days, nowadays, this semester, this year, this week

Unit 5 *Food*

Lesson A

Language Link: The simple present

Use the simple present to talk about: • facts • habits and schedules

Positive statements			Negative statements			
I You We They	speak study teach	English.	I You We They	do not don't	speak	English.
He She	speaks studies teaches		He She	does not doesn't		

Irregular forms

I go	to school
He goes	at 7:30.
I have	eggs for
She has	breakfast.
I do	homework at
He does	the library.

Lesson B

Language Link: Simple present—*yes/no* questions and short answers

Do	I you we they	speak study teach	English?
Does	he she		

Yes,	I you we they	do.
	he she	does.

No,	I you we they	don't.
	he she	doesn't.

Unit 6 *My Family*

Language Link: Possessives

Showing possession with *'s*

singular noun + *'s*	Taylor is Emily's brother. Louis's wife is Carol.	Taylor is Emily's brother. her Louis's wife is Carol. His
plural noun + '	My parents' house is big.	My parents' house is big. Their
irregular plural noun + *'s*	The children's names are Taylor and Emily.	The children's names are Taylor and Emily. Their

Emily and Taylor's father.	with two or more people, add *'s* to the final noun

Unit 7 *Time*

Lesson A

Language Link: Prepositions of time–*in/on/at*; question word *when*

When is your class?	It's on Monday. on Tuesday night. on the weekend.	*on* + day(s) of the week
	It's at 8 o'clock. at 1:30. at noon.	*at* + specific time
	It's in the morning. in the afternoon. in the evening.	*in* + time period of the day
	It's at night.	Note the exception.

Grammar Notes

Lesson B

Language Link: The simple present–*wh*-questions

Wh-questions

Where	do you	go	to college?	(I go to) N.Y.U.
	does she			(She goes to) N.Y.U.
What	do you	study?	(I study) history.	
	does she		(She studies) history.	
What	do you	do	on the weekend?	I study.
	does she			She studies.
What time	do you	have	class?	(I have class) at 10:00.
	does she			(She has class) at 10:00.
Who	do you	study with?	(I study with) my classmates.	
	does she		(She studies with) her classmates.	
With whom	do you	study?	(I study with) my classmates.	

*Note: In everyday speaking, it is more common to use *who* than *whom*.

Unit 8 *Special Occasions*

Lesson A

Language Link: Prepositions of time–*in* and *on*

| I was born in October. | Use *in* + month, year, or season. |
| in 1984. | |
in the autumn.	
I was born on October 11, 1984.	Use *on* + specific date or day
on the 11th of October.	
on Tuesday, the eleventh.	
Many restaurants are open on New Year's Eve.	

Lesson B

Language Link: *How long;* prepositions of time

With *be*	When is the movie?	It's at 7:00. It's **from** 7:00 **to** 9:00.
	How long is it?	It's **from** 7:00 **to** 9:00. (It's **for**) two hours.
With other verbs	When do you study?	(I usually study) **on** Saturday. (I usually study) **from** 5:00 **to** 6:00.
	How long do you study?	(I usually study) **from** 5:00 **to** 6:00. **for** an hour.

Unit 9 *Person to Person*

Lesson A

Language Link: Frequency adverbs

Frequency adverbs tell how often something happens.

With
be
	Jackie is **always** late for class. *100%*
	        usually
	        often
	        sometimes
	        hardly ever / seldom
	        never *0%*
		She isn't **usually** on time for class.	With *be*,
			frequency adverbs
			are after the verb.

With other verbs	Jackie **always** gets up at 8:00.	She doesn't **usually** get up at 7:00.	With other verbs, frequency adverbs are in front of the main verb.

Lesson B

Language Link: *Wh-*questions about the subject

Wh- questions about the subject

Who works for Toyota?	I do. Mr. Watanabe does.
Who speaks French?	I do. Jane does.
What flies in the air?	A plane does.
What comes after 10?	11 does.

Grammar Notes

Unit 10 *Home Sweet Home*

Lesson A

Language Link: *There is/there are; how many . . . ?*

There's a table in the dining room.
There isn't a table in the bedroom.
 	
There are chairs in the living room.
There aren't any chairs in the kitchen.
	Is there a table in the kitchen?
	    Yes, **there is.**
	    No, **there isn't.**
	
	Are there two chairs in the living room?
	Are there any chairs in the living room?
	    Yes, **there are.**
	    No, **there aren't.**
		Use *there is / there are* to:
		
		• say that something exists or doesn't exist
		• talk about location; to say where something is or is not

How many chairs are there in the dining room?	**There's** one. **There are** four. **There aren't any.**

Lesson B

Language Link: Verb + preposition

	verb	prep	noun		verb	prep	noun phrase	
Jason	listens	to	music.	I	listen	to	the radio.	Many verbs in English are followed by a preposition. Some prepositions are *at, about, for, to, with.*
Mary	is talking	to	her.	They	are talking	about	their trip.	A noun, pronoun, or noun phrase follows the preposition.

Unit 11 *Clothing*

Lesson B

Language Link: Count and noncount nouns

In English, there are **count nouns** and **noncount nouns**.

Count Nouns		Noncount Nouns
singular	plural	
an earring	two earrings	jewelry
a ring	three rings	money
a dollar	two dollars	clothing
a cent	fifteen cents	
a shirt	three shirts	Noncount nouns don't have *a*, *an*, or a number in front of the noun, and they are always singular.

Unit 12 *Jobs and Ambitions*

Lesson A

Language Link: Personality adjectives

What's Lisa like?	She's hardworking.	The adjectives *hardworking*, *lazy*, *funny*, etc. describe a person's personality or character.
	lazy	
	funny	
	serious	
	outgoing	
	shy	To ask about personality, use these questions
	smart	
	creative	
What are Yoshi's sisters like?	They're shy.	*What is _____ like?* *What are _____ like?*

Lesson B

Language Link: Talking about abilities—*can* and *can't*

I You We They He She	can speak French.	I You We They He She	can't speak French.

- *Can* and *can't* tell about ability. *Can* and *can't* are followed by the base form of the verb (for example, *speak, write, sing, play*).

- *Can't* is the contracted form of cannot. In everyday speech, it is more common to use *can't*.

Questions with *can* and *can't*	
Can you play the piano?	Yes, I **can.** No, I **can't.**
Who **can** speak German?	Rolf **can.**
What languages **can** Sonia speak?	(She **can** speak) English and Spanish.

Answer keys

Answers to page 16, Communication, The country and city game

1. Brasilia, 2. Spanish, 3. answers will vary, 4. Paris, France, 5. Cairo, 6. Spain, 7. answers will vary, 8. Australia, 9. Washington, D.C., 10. answers will vary, 11. answers will vary, 12. England, 13. possible answers: Shanghai, Beijing, Hong Kong, Nanjing, 14. Malaysia, 15. Colombian, 16. answers will vary, 17. Athens, 18. Norway, 19. Rome, 20. Austria, 21. answers will vary, 22. answers will vary, 23 **possible answers:** New York, California, Texas, Hawaii

Answers to page 65, Communication, Activity A

Sean Connery—Born 1930; Madonna—born 1958; Jackie Chan—born 1945; Bono—born 1960; Prince William—born 1986; Enrique Iglesias—born 1975

Answers to page 69, What's wrong?, Activity B

1. F, 2. F, 3. F, 4. T, 5. F, 6. F, 7. F, 8. F, 9. F, 10. T

Answers to page 82, When is Marty's birthday?, Activity C

Chow Yun Fat—May 18, 1955; Cameron Diaz—August 30, 1972; Jim Carrey—January 17, 1962; Yoko Ono—February 18, 1933

Answers to page 102, Culture Quiz: When and where, Activity A

1. b, 2. b, 3. b, 4. a, 5. b, 6. b

Answers to page 123, Communication, Activity B

Clothing and jewelry
100: answers will vary, 200: Rings, 300: answers will vary, 400: casual, 500: a hat, 600: pierced earrings, 700: (suggested answers) *kimono, yukata, zori,* 800: (suggested answers) Calvin Klein, Tommy Hilfiger

Money and numbers
100: 1,500, 200: answers will vary, 300: 11,700, 400: the Euro, 500: 4, 600: 2,100, 700: Canadian dollars, 800: *I don't have any money*

Colors
100: answers will vary, 200: red, 300: White, 400: green, 500: orange, 600: black, 700: Yellow, 800: *I'm sad.*